Quaker Theology

A Progressive Journal and Forum
For Discussion and Study

✤
Issue #29
✤

Summer-Fall 2016

Volume Fifteen, Number Two

Editor: Chuck Fager
Associate Editors:
Stephen W. Angell
& Ann K. Riggs

ISSN 1526-7482

All the essays in this issue are copyright © by
the respective authors,
and all rights are reserved by them.

Except where otherwise noted,
the views expressed in articles in *Quaker Theology*
are those of the authors, and not necessarily those of
the Editors, or Quaker Ecumenical Seminars in Theology.

Cover photo by Chuck Fager.

Quaker Theology, founded in 1999,
intends to publish at least twice a year.
Subscriptions: US$20 for two issues.
Individual copies/back issues: US$10 each, postpaid. From:

Quaker Theology
Post Office Box 3811
Durham NC 27702

Print copies of this issue can be ordered from:
www.createspace.com

Quaker Theology is also published in an online edition, at:
www.quakertheology.org

ISBN: 978-1537596563

Articles, reviews and letters are welcome.
Authors please send queries first, to the Editor
at the address above.
Or by E-mail at:
qkrtheology@gmail.com

Contents

Editor's Introduction, v

The Influence of Psychoanalysis and Popular Psychology on Quaker Thought & Practice: An Exploratory Survey. By Jacob Stone, 1

Narrative Theology: The Land. By Ken Bradstock, 17

Whittaker Chambers, Alger Hiss, and Quaker Leadership: A Problem for Friends. By H. Larry Ingle, 33

Back From The Brink: North Carolina Yearly Meeting Says No To A Split. By Chuck Fager, 50

Attachments: Documents associated with the North Carolina Yearly Meeting's Recent Actions, 59

Reviews

Our Life is Love: The Quaker Spiritual Journey. Marcelle Martin.
Reviewed by Chuck Fager, 79

Quiet Heroes: A Century of American Quakers' Love and Help for the Japanese and Japanese-Americans. Tsukasa Sugimura.
Reviewed by Chuck Fager, 85

About the Contributors, 88

Editor's Introduction

There's some good news in American Quakerdom this fall: North Carolina Yearly Meeting (FUM), whose travails we have been following for two years, has decided not to split, and the two-year effort to purge its handful of "liberal" meetings has been given up. Instead, as our report here shows, it will undertake to "reorganize" in an as-yet unspecified way, but along lines which will give room to the factions which have difficulty with other perspectives, but without pushing anyone out of the group.

This process is not yet underway as we go to press, and it will be intriguing to watch. So while NCYM's decision could well be a landmark, our coverage of NCYM is not thereby concluded.

From another sector of Friends we also have what we believe is an important piece, by liberal Friend Jacob Stone. He raises the curtain on a well-established phenomenon in this constituency, yet one that is hardly ever remarked on, except in passing: the pervasive influence of pop psychology and the morphing of "spirituality" (also previously known as "religion") into a kind of therapy equivalent.

Evangelical Friends have their own versions of this; but Stone is more familiar with liberal Quakers, and that's where he takes us. And, Friends, it's a jungle out there. (Just kidding! Really it's the Elysian Fields; it's a "safe space"; the Tunnel to Transformation; the Home of true Healing, the Bower of Breathful Bliss, etc.) In any case, under the capacious umbrella of Friends General Conference, on the verdant lawns of Pendle Hill, or Friendly spaces subject to their influence, it's well-nigh inescapable.

Stone draws back from passing any judgments about this condition. This editor is not so reluctant. I've been troubled more than once by what I've seen and heard in such settings. For one thing, much of this stuff makes at least a stab at being scientific. But a great deal is just not. Beyond my own experience and observation, I'm persuaded by the careful analysis of available research as of about 2013 by Monica Pignotti, PhD & Bruce A. Thyer, PhD, LCSW, BCBA-D, both from the College of Social Work, Florida State University, Tallahassee, Florida. In the book *Science & Pseudo-science in Clinical Psychology,* they write in "New Age & Related Novel Unsupported Therapies in Mental Health Practice":

> "Currently, conventional science has yet to validate the core principles of New Age psychotherapies – the idea that that thoughts can influence one's external environment, the existence of subtle energies and fields–or of meridians, acupressure points, chakras, auras, or of the ability of some psychotherapists to reliably detect these constructs."
> It is rare that the books, training workshops, CDs, or DVDs advertising training in these treatments, or offering them to the public . . . include a disclaimer along the lines of 'The treatment being promoted lacks an adequate scientific evidence that it is an effective therapy. It is offered solely on the basis of the psychologist's clinical judgment, intuition, and personal beliefs.'"

Further, as Pignoti and Thyer add, some of these techniques and associated paraphernalia have also proved to be downright dangerous:

> "Recall the confident assertion of one mental health professional who claimed, 'I am a sensitive observer, and my conclusion is that a vast majority of my patients get better as opposed to worse after treatment.' This professional was a psychiatrist who provided crude lobotomies on the brains of persons with mental illness during the 1950s . . . . It is now evident that prefrontal lobotomies are an ineffective treatment for persons with mental illness and in many instances are seriously injurious . . . . Offering a New Age or NUST (Novel Unsupported Therapy) to a client, when the psychologist is aware that the proffered treatment lacks credible scientific evidence of its effectiveness, and when other psychosocial or medical interventions with

a stronger evidentiary foundation exist, raises troubling ethical questions." (pp. 204f)

Long after lobotomies were discredited, there were all the variations on repressed recovered memories of trauma and abuse, which wreaked havoc far and wide, producing false prosecutions, breaking up families and making many clients worse off. As an eminent Harvard Psychology professor, Richard J. McNally, put it in a brief for one of the many lawsuits involving these "techniques":

> "The notion that traumatic events can be repressed and later recovered is the most pernicious bit of folklore ever to infect psychology and psychiatry. It has provided the theoretical basis for 'recovered memory therapy' – the worst catastrophe to befall the mental health field since the lobotomy era."

But lay all this aside. What troubles me most is the extent to which this yeasty, faddish mishmash of "novel unsupported (by scientific research) therapies" has progressively absorbed and often seems to essentially displace religion in many Quaker settings: you know, the actual experience and evolution of an existing faith community, plus the people, saints and villains, who shaped it. This also includes theology (even for non-theists), scriptures, the study and grappling therewith, not to mention actual (rather than legendary/mythical) relationships to other religions.

Our hope is that Jacob Stone's beginning glimpse of all this can stimulate more re-examination and candid discussion among liberal Friends about this situation.

Speaking of history and overdue re-examinations, Quaker historian H. Larry Ingle brings back to light a now-forgotten incident which was pivotal in the shaping of American public and political culture in the early Cold War, and what is still called McCarthyism. But he isn't doing this simply to rehearse somebody else's story, but rather to retrieve an episode in which Quakers, and Friendly fellow-travelers, were integrally involved. It centers on the trial of Alger Hiss, a rising Washington insider who had been very involved with key Quaker groups in Philadelphia. In 1948 Hiss was accused of being a Communist spy, by Whittaker Chambers, a previously obscure writer for *TIME* Magazine. Hiss wound up in jail, and

Chambers then published a massively best-selling memoir, *Witness*, which described not only his own Communist spy past, and the Hiss trial, but also his convincement and entry into the Society of Friends.

In the tumultuous aftermath of this case, how did the Philadelphia Quaker establishment of Philadelphia deal with these revelations and with Chambers, who had brought them to light? Well, turn to Ingle's article to find out; the answer is important and disturbing.

And then for a more directly personal human story, we have a narrative theology piece by Ken Bradstock, tracing his religious evolution from rock-ribbed fundamentalist Christianity into the Marines, the Sheriff's office, and after more turns, to Quakerism, and then more. It's been two years since we published a comparable narrative essay, and it's good to be able to add this to our series.

Two book reviews wrap up this packed issue. *Our Life Is Love* is a new overview of what author Marcelle Martin considers the key elements of Quaker religious development. Then there's a very different story, *Quiet Heroes*, which brings back from obscurity a very telling episode from World War Two: the internment of 120,000 Japanese-Americans in what were essentially domestic concentration camps. The author is a descendant of internees, yet he wrote this book less to tell that sad and outrageous story, than as a tribute to the group that did more at the time to minister to the prisoners and advocate for their release than any oher white outsiders: Friends.

– Chuck Fager

The Influence of Psychoanalysis and Popular Psychology
on Quaker Thought & Practice:
An Exploratory Survey

Jacob Stone

One Saturday back in the early 1990's I found myself in a brief workshop sponsored by a Quaker organization; there was a short business meeting, a presentation, some socialization and networking during "dinner on the grounds". And then…..
…..a program about how I could "heal" myself. I didn't at that time feel any particular need for healing, but I was told that by understanding the social and familial forces that have plagued me (and, supposedly, everyone) I could begin to resolve my issues and heal. I was then offered the opportunity to work with another workshop participant to share our history, our pain and our strivings so we could each find the "divine" person within. I participated, because it seemed harmless if a bit feckless, and my partner was clearly enthusiastic about it all; I thought perhaps I could be of some support to him even if I was more than a little skeptical.

Well, I don't think I was any more divine or healed that day than I was before this episode of amateur psychotherapy, but I came away with the beginnings of an interest and inquiry that I've followed for the past quarter-century: the impact of psychoanalytic thought and new age/pop psychology (let's conflate it all as PNAP) on Quaker thought and practice. Tracing it has been an interesting journey. For me, it is more than a passing interest or hobby. My sense is that some of the overarching themes of PNAP have changed Quaker thought and practice, for better or worse.

I've been an active Friend for over forty years, mostly at the level of my monthly and quarterly meeting and Friends General Conference. I've attended 32 of the past 33 Friends General Conference Gatherings. I've served twice as a Friend in Residence (once at Pendle Hill, once at a meeting). I have worked as an executive for a Friends organization, and have visited meetings throughout North America facilitating couple enrichment retreats with my wife. I've served on more Friends' committees and boards than I can remember, and in my professional capacity have consulted with a number of Friends organizations and facilities. This exhausting Quaker resume has been an immensely rich opportunity over the years to observe Friends functioning in many Quaker contexts. It has been a wonderful opportunity to explore my interest in the impact of PNAP on Friends thought and practice. I've been helped in this by my professional life, in which I've been a counselor, consultant, administrator and teacher in a wide range of mental health, business and university settings.

Before I proceed let me sharpen the focus of this inquiry. I want to be clear about who I'm talking about when I describe "Quakers". Many of my observations in preparing this paper have been *in vivo* during my years as a Friend, and by that I mean the liberal, unprogrammed tradition of Quakerism that generally falls under the umbrella of Friends General Conference. I have no experience with programmed meetings or evangelical Friends churches, nor have I done any significant research about them, so I am limiting my observations to the species of Quaker that I know: the liberal, unprogrammed tradition.

I also want to be clear about what I'm talking about when I refer to "psychology". The psychology that I want to explore is that which has reached and impacted the popular culture, and not necessarily the professional practice of psychology, psychiatry, etc. (although there is clearly some overlap here). From their earliest days the mental health professions have marched along, progressing in fits and starts, doing important research, and often being of real help to people. There has always been a core of thoughtful professionals whose work is effective, ethical, and not impacted by popular fads. What I want to address in this paper is the psychological thought that has become part of our popular culture, and thus impacted Quaker thought and practice.

* * *

To put all of this into context we should briefly look at the way that cultural "landmarks" can exert massive influence on a popular culture. Sometimes seemingly minor and time-limited events can change a social context if they happen to find fertile ground for this change. For example, the opening of the tomb of Tutankhamen in 1923 ignited a furor of interest in Egypt; the 1970's television show "Kung Fu" was a catalyst for an explosion of interest in eastern religion, philosophy and martial arts.

In the world of PNAP there have also been these bellwether events. One that is particularly relevant to this inquiry is a lecture series by Freud and Jung in 1909 that ignited an intense interest in psychoanalytic concepts. (More about this a bit later.) Another one was the publication in 1988 of "The Courage to Heal", a pivotal catalyst for a terrifying mania suggesting that millions of people had been subjected to parental sexual abuse but had repressed all memory of it.

It is naïve to think that Friends culture is in any way immune to these influences. Despite the 18th, 19th and early 20th century effort to provide a "guarded" education and social context for Friends the popular culture inevitably found its way in. By the mid 20th century efforts to maintain these barriers were anachronistic artifacts rather than serious efforts.(1) Music, dance, attending secular schools and colleges, marrying outside the faith, all became acceptable. Even couples from the two factions of the Hicksite-Orthodox schism were permitted to wed and reproduce, *mirabile dictu*.

The two thematic wellsprings that I believe have influenced Quaker thought and practice are the psychoanalytic movement that began in America in 1909, and the New Age/pop psychology movement that began in earnest in the years after WWII and continues unabated through today, conflated here as PNAP. Although the two schools differ dramatically in philosophy and technique, and haven't always gotten along well with each other, there are some enduring commonalities which I believe have had a significant impact on Friends.

The psychoanalytic movement in America has a specific birthday: September 7, 1909, when Sigmund Freud gave the first of several lectures at Clark University in Massachusetts. From the vantage point of the 21st century it is hard for us to understand the massive and enduring impact of these (and related) lectures. Psychoanalytic concepts and terminology filtered into the daily discourse of American society. Popular magazines wrote breathlessly about it, asserting that it would be the method by which the world's ills would be cured.

Even today, concepts such as ego, id, repression, catharsis, neurosis, the unconscious, resistance, and myriad others are so immured in our language that we've lost sight of their origins. Undergoing psychoanalysis came to be seen as a journey to wellness and wholeness, a "transformative" journey that would require courage, perseverance, and a lot of money; a typical analysis involved four or five sessions a week for several years. (More about "transformation a bit later.)

From its earliest days some pivotal themes have been integral to the psychoanalytic movement, and they are important to identify here:

> • First and foremost, psychoanalysis was (and is) about **the individual**, with little attention to the person as part of a social network or system. Any interest in others was only in regard to their possible impact or damage on the individual.
> When I was first studying psychology back in the early 1970's I came upon the topic of "object relations". At first I thought it might refer to how I got along with my desk or my typewriter, but I soon learned that the "objects" were other people in the life of the individual. The psychoanalytic

patient was in effect in a one-person drama, with all other characters playing bit parts, or off-stage parts. Although the psychoanalytic movement grew within the context of the European Enlightenment that recognized individual rights and dignity, this new movement added a narcissistic/ solipsistic element. A psychoanalytic process was not couples counseling, family therapy or group therapy. It was an intense one-on-one process between an analysand and an opaque analyst.

• Psychoanalytic theory was also **about the past, and often about blaming others**. Childhood experiences, and especially alleged parental misfeasance, were often considered to be the source of problematic behaviors and attitudes in adulthood. Mothers were popular targets of psychoanalysts, and until the 1970's schizophrenia and autism were thought to be caused by "schizophrenegenic" mothers. The damage caused by this idea was dredful.

• **The idea that a "better" self was hidden within the individual** was a key tenet of psychoanalysis. The goal has always been to uncover and encourage this better individual through this "hero's journey". The "hero" would ostensibly go on to live a more self-aware and more fulfilled life, a transformed life.

• Freud and those who followed him articulated the idea of the **unconscious**, with drives and motivations that might not be readily known and understood by the individual. A key part of the psychoanalytic process was the discovery and exploration of these repressed elements of the person.

It's not hard for Friends to see how and why psychoanalytic thought resonated with our testimonies. A psychoanalytic process is not unlike the ongoing labor with our testimonies that many Friends try to undertake in search of rightly ordered living. Religious or psychotherapeutic? It may be that they differ only in that one of them includes a deity in its discourse. I'm reminded of an old joke by Woody Allen: he told of a conflict with the IRS when he tried to deduct the cost of his psychoanalysis as a medical expense. The IRS countered that it should be considered entertainment; they finally compromised and made it a religious contribution.

This is only a brief and superficial description of key psychoanalytic concepts, but it summarizes the ideas that have permeated our culture since that day in 1909, and they have instructed and informed the popular psychology and self-help movements of the years since WWII. Read on for more about this.

* * *

In the years after WWII the various mental health fields began to shake loose from the ascendancy of psychoanalytic thought that dominated in the first half of the 20th century. Some have called the new thinking "pop" psychology; others have referred to it as New Age Psychology. At the risk of infuriating one or another acolyte of a particular psychological idiom we can effectively conflate them here to include the various ideas about psychology that became part of the popular culture and which played the same role in postwar years that psychoanalytic thought played earlier in the century.

So, exactly what is this "Pop/New Age" psychology? Its scope overlaps with more clinical psychology and psychiatry, and often refers to a "spiritual" component. We find the fingerprints of PNAP in therapeutic practices, in myriad self-help programs, and in a vast library of self-help books. A comprehensive list of these PNAP initiatives would more than fill this journal, but here are a few notable ones:

- gestalt therapy
- est
- primal scream therapy
- bioenergetics
- thought field therapy
- emotional freedom technique
- therapeutic touch
- rebirthing
- EMDR
- repressed memory therapy
- past life regression
- Enneagram
- Myers-Briggs Types
- Scientology, in its focus on "auditing" to achieve a "clear" state

And the self-help groups and 12 Step Programs

- Alcoholics Anonymous
- Narcotics Anonymous
- Co-Dependents Anonymous
- Neurotics Anonymous
- Survivors of Incest Anonymous
- Schizophrenics Anonymous
- Emotions Anonymous

….and myriad more

And the books:

- *Looking Out for Number One*
- *How to be Your Own Best Friend*
- *The Seven habits of Highly Effective People*
- *Getting Unstuck*
- *The Power of Now: A guide to spiritual enlightenment* (talks about dealing with the false self)
- *Predictably Irrational: The Hidden Forces that Shape our Decisions*
- *You Can Heal Your Life*
- *Codependent No More*
- *The Courage to Heal*
- *Awaken the Giant Within: How to Take Immediate Control of Your Mental, Emotional, Physical and Financial Destiny!*
- *There is Nothing Wrong with You: Going Beyond Self-hate*
- *The Power of Your Subconscious Mind*
- *I'm OK, You're OK*
- *Learned Optimism: How to Change your Mind and Your Life*

The overarching themes of PNAP clearly borrow from the psychoanalytic movement, and expand on them. It is important to remember that Freud was ambivalent at best about the therapeutic benefits of his processes; he saw it as a process of self-exploration that might have some growth potential for analysands. It was his followers and later the acolytes of PNAP that painted their initiatives as manifestly therapeutic. If we can generalize about PNAP (a difficult task, since the boundaries of all this are fuzzy) we find some distinctive themes that echo psychoanalysis in many ways:

- A **solitary and even solipsistic focus** that often ignores relationships and responsibilities to others; books such as "Looking Out for Number One" and "How to Be Your Own Best Friend" are iconic examples of this. A famous text, "Codependent No More", pathologizes our strong feelings about others. I remember serving on a clearness committee many years ago in which an engaged couple was seriously at odds because one of them was deeply concerned about his aging father; his spouse accused him of being "codependent", when in fact it seemed to me that the son's concern about his father was simply the love that a child can feel for a parent. The couple struggled to reconcile the perspective of "codependency" with the testimony of stewardship that was guiding the son to seek ways to support his father.

The apotheosis of this solitary focus comes from Fritz Perls, the father of Gestalt Therapy, who wrote that "I am not in this world to live up to other people's expectations, nor do I feel that the world must live up to mine." He also asserted that "Our dependency makes slaves out of us, especially if this dependency is a dependency of our self-esteem. If you need encouragement, praise, pats on the back from everybody, then you make everybody your judge."

• A **reframing of feelings of self-blame, shame or guilt, even if justified, as a psychological problem or deficit**, ignoring, minimizing or explaining away actual behaviors that should reasonably generate feelings of shame. The inevitable corollary to this was a more individually centered and self-generated set of moral standards, far different from the moral standards set by Friends testimonies or other cultural moral standards. The massive juggernaut of 12 step programs–Alcoholics Anonymous and its countless spinoffs –are all based on the idea that an important first step in recovery is to acknowledge a powerless stance in regard to whatever issue is troubling them. The removal of shame thus becomes the first step in regaining power.

• **The belief that many of our behaviors and difficulties are caused by forces outside our conscious awareness,** and that we can access this "subconscious. Accessing and understanding this "subconscious" has been central to both psychoanalysis and PNAP, with the hope that bringing this into conscious awareness will allow us to change for the better. (O how I wish this were true; I am unalterably beset with lots of issues that hobble me, even though I am painfully aware of their source and meaning; many people would surely say the same about themselves.)

• **The possibility of transformation through technique** has also been a cornerstone of psychoanalysis and PNAP. The various luminaries of the psychoanalytic movement have argued for over a century over arcane elements of technique, and the discourse continues unabated today. PNAP has spawned countless techniques, each initially claiming to be a "holy grail" of transformation. A complete list of these would fill this journal, but here are a few of the better known technique-based approaches: Neuro-Linguistic Programming; EMDR, Thought Field Therapy, Dianetics (from the Church of Scientology), hypnotherapy, Bioenergetics, repressed memory therapy, Primal Scream Therapy. The list is endless, with new techniques being spawned every day.

These themes in and of themselves have been critiqued, analyzed and defended for decades, and there's no need here to add to those conversations. For our purposes I simply want to record their presence in our culture and describe their most distinctive features, so we can see what impact if any they have had on Quaker thought and practice.

* * *

Some Thoughts About Transformation

Before we continue, the topic of "transformation" needs some further examination here. It is arguably one of the most overused words in the Quaker lexicon (along with "deep"). Its meaning is fuzzy at best, and can mean different things to different people, but the influence of PNAP may have given it a new meaning. It is important to examine it because it is often a key component of PNAP activities.

The concept of "transformation" in and of itself is a venerable theme in religious tales, generally meaning that a person underwent a sudden change that led to a connection with the divine and a sense of belonging to the divine. The story of Saul of Tarsus is the ur- narrative of transformation, but we can also find it in the story of Francis of Assisi and St. Augustine's "transformation" from wild child to theologian. Televangelists tell us of the number of souls they have saved at mass rallies. We sometimes hear messages in meeting for worship of someone suddenly having found a new identity, a new purpose, a new motivation. This is often characterized as "transformation", and it seems like a reasonable use of the word. Its defining characteristics are suddenness and a manifestly religious content.

I myself have been transformed, but it has been a much slower and less dramatic process. It has taken all of the forty years I have spent among Friends, and continues today. The process of my transformation has been based on my decades of laboring with some of our testimonies, most notably those of simplicity and stewardship. I've also been helped along by exemplars and role models, some real and some not (Henry Cadbury, Walt Whitman and Jean-Luc Picard to name just three of many.) It can be called transformation, and I credit Doylestown Friends Meeting and the wider world of Friends among the authors of this transformation. But it can just as easily be seen as a process of maturing, evolving, studying, and observing. This sort of transformation is an evolutionary process that encompasses all aspects of my life. The more cloistered life of Friends in the 18th and 19th centuries was perhaps a way to manage this sort of transformation and guide it in a specific direction.

But in the world of PNAP the idea of transformation has become more complex and fungible, and it seems to be used without any consistent referents. Sometimes it refers to a sense of self-awareness, which is a common goal of analytic processes; other times it refers to happiness, freedom from pain, financial prosperity, or better sleep. One popular PNAP technique, the Emotional Freedom Technique, promises that

> Instead of taking months or years with conventional counseling, EFT can fast track results down to even one or two sessions. Positive results are literally experienced within minutes of beginning the tapping. This emotional clearing soon results in the fading of physical pain and discomfort. The symptoms may even vanish altogether.
>
> Emotional Freedom Technique also has the ability to change negative belief systems about ourselves that limit our potential and prevent us from living the life we deserve. If you have heard of The Secret and The Law of Attraction, then EFT is a huge part of this consciousness movement because it has the power to transform the subconscious mind so effectively and quickly. (2)

There are endless other examples of programs that offer one form or another of a vaguely defined quick fix that is often characterized as "transformation", each with its own definition of this transformative outcome. The descriptors are usually vague and universal concepts such as "the end of suffering", happiness, calm, or self-awareness. But regardless of the particular nature of the promise that is given, the key elements for our purposes are that there is the application of a **technique,** there is the hope or expectation of a **quick change,** and the possibility that **the transformation may not be expressly religious or spiritual.** The venerable psychoanalytic techniques promised this as the product of a long and expensive process; the techniques of more modern popular psychology offer a much faster approach. These techniques are perhaps secular versions of the "blinding revelations" of religious mystics. However, while some of these PNAP techniques seem manifestly absurd, it is impossible to make any overarching evaluation of them; people are helped and even" transformed" by all sorts of approaches.

In the final analysis the promiscuous use of the word "transformation" leaves me without any coherent understanding of what it means. We can make some general observations about it all, but ultimately those who offer "transformation" should be able to explain what they are offering, and those who seek it should first understand the specific components of what they are seeking.

That having been noted, we can begin to look at what has actually been happening among Friends in regard to PNAP.

* * *

A word about methodology here. Liberal Quakerism is marked by a distinctive lack of any central arbiter of doctrine and practice. Even though each yearly meeting publishes its own book of Faith and Practice our congregational nature leaves, and even encourages, each meeting to develop its own culture. In my travels through the corridors of Quakerism over the last forty years I've been astonished at what a heterogeneous sect we have become. One meeting is manifestly Christian, and the next one seems to have a Universalist tilt to it. Some meetings are energized by social activism, while others seem to focus on personal introspection. Some meetings are manifestly "religious", while others are more "psychological" in their activities, committees, and messages in meeting for worship. (Some of us celebrate this heterogeneity; others of us foment schisms over it all.)

Given this, any general observation by a single person about Quaker thought and practice and about the impact of PNAP is necessarily personal, impressionistic and exploratory. These observations aren't statistically rigorous and certainly not definitive, but perhaps will serve to identify some interesting trends. More important, I hope that readers will want to consider whether and how much the emphases of PNAP in Quakerism are rightly ordered.

So, taking into consideration the limitations of this inquiry, I'm drawing some information from four sources:

- First and foremost, the workshops and programs offered at the annual Friends General Conference Gathering have been an immensely rich source of insight into this topic; their changing nature over the decades offers some valuable insights. FGC has been around for 116 years, and its annual gatherings, in various formats, are almost as venerable. This single source of comparative information has proven particularly useful. I appreciate the support of the Friends Historical Library at Swarthmore College, as well as the current staff of Friends General Conference, who provided valuable assistance in this research.

- The archived resources of *Friends Journal*, which covers all it has published for the past sixty years or more, both chronologically and by subject "tags".

- The long series of Pendle Hill Pamphlets, over four hundred of them dating back to the 1930's.

- Last, my own experiences over the past forty years in various meetings throughout the United States and the UK, and my involvement with a wide range of Friends organizations.

There are surely many other sources of information to mine, but I offer these as a starting point for any further exploration.

* * *

So, my digging around in these places has focused on when and how the themes mentioned earlier seemed to appear. In summary form these themes are:

- **a primary focus on the individual and less on the community, family or social context**
- **careful examination of the past for clues about current problems and functioning, often blaming others for difficulties and pathologies.**
- **the idea of unconscious drives and motivations as important elements of a psyche**
- **the possibility of transformation and growth through effort and application of special techniques**

* * *

Friends General Conference Gathering Workshops

It has been instructive to follow the programs and workshops offered by Friends General Conference; the years right after WWII were the first for which coherent records are available and workshops had formats somewhat comparable to what occurs today at the Gathering. There were of course a lot of programs dealing with politics, social justice, and the post WWII world. For example, in 1950 there was a "Human Relations" round table; a few years later a program on "How Shall We Act in Conflict Situations". In the early 1960's a program on "Human Values in Urban Society" was presented. At the same time there were programs that had a psychological orientation, such as "Why Do People Drink?" in 1952; "Meaningful Living in the Second Half of Life" in 1960; "Family Living" in 1962; "Finding Meaning in Everyday Encounters" in 1966; and "Family Life and Counsel" in 1967. I made note of their focus on social groups and social interaction.

The leitmotif of these psychologically oriented programs was practicality and advice about living effectively. They didn't seem to have the darker themes that we've identified as coming from PNAP ideology. They were perhaps more advisory and encouraging than therapeutic. The Couple Enrichment program that FGC sponsored for close to half a century is of this practical genre. Programs of this nature are a valuable and venerable part of the Quaker world, and we all benefit from their ongoing presence.

But in the mid to late 1960's – the time of the greatest ascendency of PNAP activities in the US–the tone of the programs at the Gathering began to shift. In 1969 a lecture on "Fulfillment and the Expansion of Consciousness" was offered. The following year a Tai Chi program was offered, entitled "Meditation in Movement". In 1972 Ira Progoff offered a program on "The Next Step in Social Consciousness". (Progoff was an analysand and student of Carl Jung; he created the Intensive Journal Method, a fountainhead of all current journaling practices; journaling as Progoff conceived it and as it is currently practiced is an entirely self-focused discipline. I would argue that it has a narcissistic flavor to it; I attended a weekend program with Progoff himself in the early 1990's, and I remember being struck by the solitary and self-focused nature of it all.)

In 1973 "Seeking Spiritual Depth through Human Potential Media" was offered, along with programs on Creative Movement and Transcendental Meditation"; 1975 offered programs on yoga, journal keeping, and something called "Reaching for Healing Strength". It is worth noting that this is the first time I encountered the idea of "healing" within a psychological context in these workshops.

In the early 1980's a program entitled "Fine Tuning", which didn't appear to be about pianos, was offered, as was "Introspective Exploration", "Ministry of Healing", "Quest for Self", "Holistic Health", "Wholeness in Life", "Journal Keeping for Spiritual Growth", and "Right Brain/Left Brain Balance for Wholeness".

It is also worth noting that during the early 1980's a number of workshops were offered relating to gender and the challenges of being male or female. A program entitled "Men's Issues" was about how gender oppresses men and women. A year later a program entitled "Men's Experience" was offered. A few years later a program about "Spiritual Survival and Spiritual Healing for Incest Survivors" was available, along with one entitled "Women's Rituals". These programs were offered at a time when charges of sexual abuse and repressed memory filled the popular media and publicity-seeking therapists–most notably John Bradshaw–were pontificating about the "holocaust" of the American family.

I remember an afternoon program at a Gathering at about that time–not a formal workshop–in which a group of presenters put forth the idea that my entire gender is made up of sexual predators. At about that same time a plenary presenter, Sonia Johnson, used her platform to denigrate and insult men–all men–for their violent, aggressive and predatory nature; she seemed to have a particular animus for Margaret Thatcher, and insulted her by calling her an "honorary man". It was shocking to see the way that these particularly potent and volatile memes from PNAP found their way into this Quaker fold.

Programs on Therapeutic Touch and something called "Friendly Touch" were offered in the late 1980's. An AA-based workshop on "Recovery" was available at that time. Other programs were "The Experience of Being a Man", "Dreams, Visions, Voices, Signs", "Re-Evaluation Counseling", "Family of Origin Issues", "Becoming Whole, Becoming Oneself", and "Building Toward Self-Reliance".

In the 1990's the trend continued, with "The Boy is the Father of The Man", "Men's Lives", "Body, Mind and Spirit" (about kinesiology), "Healing Internalized Homophobia", "Spiritual Centering Through Yoga and Meditation", "Healing from Trauma" (for couples), "Enneagram as a Spiritual Tool", and "Meeting for Worship for Healing".

In the 21st century the same themes are present: "Being Bodies and Loving It"; "Reiki Healing"; "Gifts and Callings: Discovering Ourselves"; "Past Life Exploration"; Two workshops, one for men and one for women, on "Coming to Peace Between Generations"; "Living Skillfully With Outrage" for men, and "Anger and the Third Way" for women; Overcoming Internalized Oppression"; "Creating a Personal Spiritual Fairy Tale". (It was interesting to observe at the 2016 Gathering that the workshops and plenary sessions seemed to be more focused on social justice, interactional and Quaker functioning issues, with perhaps less of an emphasis on individual issues; we'll see what the future holds in this regard.)

I want to emphasize that I'm not offering any critiques or evaluations of these programs, except perhaps for those that attacked or accused my gender, or inflamed people with absurd allegations about family members. People are helped and taught in many ways, and it is beyond my pay grade to editorialize about them. Indeed, all I mean to do here is identify the PNAP themes and the ways that may have impacted on Quaker thought and practice. I leave it to others to apply any value judgments.

Friends Journal and Pendle Hill Pamphlets

Let me now turn much more briefly to *Friends Journal* (FJ), and then to Pendle Hill. The goals and roles of FJ are broad. Much of what we find within its pages is reporting and news of yearly meetings and Friends organizations, and the activities of individual Friends. Even the articles that are manifestly about Quaker thought and practice (rather than quotidian reportage) seem to me to have a "real-world" practicality. But this approach still has a great deal of room for material that might be considered to have a psychological orientation, and it is within these articles that it is useful to seek out hints of the influence of PNAP.

The topics that FJ has discussed over the decades that might reflect PNAP's impact include marriage, parenting, sexuality, LGBTQ issues, and PTSD, among others. Most of these articles reflect the practical bent of FJ, but it is useful to note the prevalence of one "tag" in FJ's online index: the topic of **healing**, which accounted for no fewer than 64 tags covering the past fifteen years. Spelunking through these tags one finds material that clearly has some of the elements of PNAP effectively conflated with traditional Friends' ideas and discourse. "Forgiveness: A Personal Journey" appeared in 2003; an article from 2005, written by a psychologist was about "The Wounding and Healing of the Human Spirit"; "Abuse and Healing" appeared in 2008.

The multifaceted mission of FJ perhaps made the impact of PNAP less obvious than in other contexts, I guessed. But then the current (9/16) issue of FJ arrived in my mailbox. It reports at length on the current ferment at Friends General Conference and the various yearly meetings about white privilege and white supremacy. One prominent article suggests that we need a "12-step program to overcome our internalized racism". It goes on to outline these steps, some of which come directly from the memes of PNAP: "We admitted we were powerless over having been colonized by our white supremacist culture..."; "We admitted to ourselves and to another human being the exact nature of these modes of thought, action and silence"; "In humility, we let go of destructive habits..." White supremacy is characterized as "addiction and as a disease". Just as all of the many 12 step programs contain the themes of PNAP, in this FJ article we can see clearly the idea of the unconscious, the role of guilt/blame, and the possibility of transformation. It seems that the memes of PNAP have become so immured in our cultural discourse that they have taken on a self-evidentiary quality. It will be interesting to watch the progress of this important and long-overdue initiative.

Pendle Hill has published more than four hundred pamphlets since the inception of the series in 1934. From the beginning many were clearly about the practice of Quakerism, but the years surrounding WWII and the Cold War were marked by interest in peace, politics, and activism. Some acknowledgement of psychology was evident in the early years of the pamphlets, but they were of a more practical nature, as in the pamphlet on "Religion and Mental Illness, by Carol Murphy (1955), which focused on pastoral care and mental illness. But then, in the late 1960's and into the 1970's there was a spike in interest in psychological issues, many of them with distinct PNAP connections. The frequency of these diminished afterward, but with some pamphlets still featuring PNAP elements. Here are some of the titles:

- *Psychotherapy Based on Human Longing*, by Robert Murphy (1961)
- *Born Remembering*, by Elise Boulding (1975) (About childhood memories and forgetting)
- *The Psychology of a Fairy Tale*, by David Hart (1977)
- *A Quaker Looks at Yoga*, by Dorothy Ackerman (1976)

- *Seeking Light in the Darkness of the Unconscious*, by John Yungblut (1977)
- *The Unconscious,* by Robert Murphy (1996)
- *Depression and Spiritual Growth*, by Dimitri Mihalas (1996)
- *Living from the Center: Mindfulness Meditation and Centering for Friends*, by Valerie Brown, 2010

Some Personal Experiences and Observations

I've been fortunate in the past forty years to visit many Friends Meetings throughout the country. While each meeting has its own culture the element of silent unprogrammed worship has been consistent and welcoming for me. After all, how much variety can there be in a room with Friends sitting in silence? Well, in the past decade (or thereabouts) I've observed two changes in the ways that meetings for worship are conducted, and these changes seem to reflect some of the themes I've identified.

One of these changes is the increasingly common practice of asking, once meeting for worship has ended, if anyone has something they would like to share that "did not rise to the level of a message in meeting for worship". The other change is the very common practice of the clerk asking if there are any requests for the meeting to "hold someone in the light", a Quaker-style request for intercessory prayer.

What often follows when these opportunities are given can seem reminiscent of a 12 step program or a group therapy session. Confessions, expressions of guilt or anger, reports of new insights, and delving into the past for answers, all seem to be common in these post-meeting discussions. They don't particularly feel right for me, but then they may be powerful additions to Quaker worship for others. I'm prepared to withhold judgment.

I've also observed during the past forty years that the nature of clearness committees, meeting support groups and even Friends gatherings has shifted toward the psychological. What was often the role of meeting elders when I first connected with Friends has become the role of Friends who can offer some professional counseling expertise; I have been asked many times to serve on clearness or support committees solely because of my professional background.

There are other markers of this infusion of PNAP themes: The Friends Conference on Religion and Psychology (http://fcrp.quaker.org), an annual event which began in 1943, has as part of its mission "to discover our own deepest processes and nourish them... (and to)...uncover the ways in which our new insights can help us return to the everyday world more focused and grounded in our spiritual reality" (3); there is the theme of transformation in purest form, with slightly different words.

Couple Enrichment, which began as a peer program many years ago, now has an extensive training and recognition program, and many leader couples who are mental health professionals. At least one yearly meeting maintains a Friends counseling service. Friends' gatherings often offer the availability of professional counselors, or healing centers, or "safety net" programs to deal with emotional issues that arise in the course of a gathering. 12 step programs are common at these gatherings, offering support for a wide variety of struggles and issues. The DNA of PNAP is everywhere in our religious community.

* * *

So, in the final analysis, it seems that PNAP has found its way into Friends thought and practice, and this may not be either all good or all bad. The focus of PNAP on the individual, the displacement of guilt, shame and blame, and the offer of possible sudden transformation seem to have had some direct impact on the way we think and function as Friends. This is a worthwhile topic for Friends to consider, and for them to evaluate whether these shifts are rightly ordered.

Quakerism continues to evolve, and our congregational nature perhaps makes us particularly open to (vulnerable to?) the influence of social trends in popular culture. Our cherished identity as a "peculiar" and isolated people is by now largely myth, and it is useful for us to be aware of how we are being influenced. We have the opportunity to embrace or challenge these changes, and that discernment is best made with some conscious awareness of what is influencing us.

NOTES

1. A fascinating novel about this is *The Bulwark*, Theodore Dreiser's last novel. Its protagonist, Rufus Barnes, is modeled on Rufus Jones; the novel describes Barnes' failed efforts to maintain a "bulwark" against modern culture. Dreiser and Jones knew each other, and Dreiser's portrayal of Quakerism in the early 20th century is insightful and accurate.

2. Conscious Wealth Institute,
   http://consciouswealthinstitute.com/about-emotional-freedom-technique-eft/

3. http://fcrp.quaker.org/

Narrative Theology: The Land

Ken Bradstock

On the Appalachian Plateau in Southwestern Pennsylvania, a farm lies fallow from decades of disuse. The fine old Pennsylvania bank barn has collapsed toward the silo. The roof is lying on the wooden ruins and they in turn have buckled and fainted onto the stone work foundation. The pastures and crop fields all across that mountain have gone to weeds, then to scrub and are now returning to the hardwood cleared before the French and Indian War.

This fate was to be expected especially from the people who bought that precious piece of history from my family. With little respect for the land and the farm, they found a way to paste modernization obscenely onto the old log and clapboard house with some sort of glass sun room. They tore down the high front porch leaving the exterior of the sun room hanging out the front wall like a silicone wart. Then for some unimaginable reason, they allowed Aunt Myrtle's beautiful yard to grow into a briar patch that obscures the view of the house from that old country road.

As far back as age 5, I loved that farm. Aunt Myrtle taught flannel graph Bible stories for kids in her front room around the large coal stove and our knees lined up on the sofa that smelled of farm animals and my unwashed Uncle Joe. She led me to Christ in that living room the year I was 5 and it is an event firmly ensconced in my mind until this day. It always amazes me as to how those salvation events are so entrenched in the minds of people who experience them. They call it "Salvation" but in my life-long study of religion and its psychology, it is very similar to almost every significant religious awakening. I have a very clear picture of her, the living room, the kids on the sofa and the act of raising my hand. She asked if anybody wanted the "New Man" to run their lives instead of the "Old Man." It was a teaching from St Paul and is a piece of good solid Evangelical Orthodoxy.

I loved Aunt Myrtle, but over the years, I realized that this was more than the family tie of being my paternal grandmother's sister. It was her close bond to something that I loved far more but took years of excavating to identify. No relative in my family livery aside from my father held my esteem more strongly. It has also come to me that I associate my love for her with my love for the land.

I hesitate to begin a description of her here because of my temptation to become romantically entangled with my love for both. Snapshots will do for now: her at the churn, or with the bell that brought the hands in from the field for dinner, or the burdened table piled with her produce cooked all morning, and her stained apron and long white hair tied in a bun. These shots capture her sweet demeanor, but they also peek at the shadow of a woman who spent a life-time with a drunken, abusive husband. The chickens were hers; the kitchen garden was hers along with the rhubarb and the apples. The tomatoes Uncle Joe grew in perfect red and green rows out of black soil also ended up somewhere in the symphony of her table.

Aunt Myrtle knew the history of the farm and would tell stories about the part it played as she cared for the flowers she always planted around the huge grindstone in the front yard. It was there I learned about the Whiskey Rebellion of 1791, not in a classroom. She could show a kid the gun ports in the logs used to fight the French and Indians, and tell the story of the stone safe room under the house she used for a root cellar. That damp room encased in stone would be filled with family and livestock when an Indian attack was anticipated. The house could be burned to the ground and those in the stony vault would be protected. Her work and her life were tied to the land, and my love for the land and the farm were teamed with a child's awe for her.

Her eyes would light up when I and my cousin Don helped collect eggs or pick up apples over near the barn for a pie or two or three. She had a look of pleasure when she made us take over the churning while she checked on something. It was fun for her to tease us when a few minutes of pumping would have both of us panting and sweating compared to her ease and rhythm.

I wasn't aware that the land was sick where we lived. I was less than a year old in late October of 1948 when the Donora Steel mills, American Steel and Wire Works and Carnegie Steel poured sulfuric acid, soluble sulphants, and fluorides into the air.

Along with this industry there were also coal burning locomotives and river boats pushing barges up and down the Monongahela River. There had been complaints from citizens for years but the Carnegies and the Mellons were able to keep up their manufacturing practices regardless of the extreme damage that was done to the environment and the people of the Monongahela Valley.

On October 30 and 31st of 1948, a weather inversion drew attention to the struggle to breathe in the area. It was a normal phenomenon wherein cold air trapped warm air in the valley like a lid. It was deadly because there was no movement of air in the area to blow the cool air away and allow the warm air to escape. That inversion remained for several days, forcing the toxins down to the ground. In the first 24 hours, 19 people died from the pollution and many more died from it later; suffered long-term disease and early death for decades after the incident. It killed pets in large numbers.

But it wasn't just the incident of the Donora Smog. I remember distinctly the black filth that gathered on everything and the reddened air, we called "Mill Dirt." When the Zinc Works was running full on, the odor of the pollutants and the filth saturated everything. Farmers who tried to pasture on the ridges around the mills complained that nothing would grow and the land became useless. My parents began looking for a way to get the family out of that rust belt town, and they finally moved us to Philadelphia.

An ever present part of my homeland, water and rivers meant more to me than I knew. When an undergraduate course in literature at Winston-Salem State University revealed the master Langston Hughes to me. I was spellbound by his poem, "The Negro Speaks of Rivers" (Hughes, 1994).

> *I've known rivers:*
> *I've known rivers ancient as the world and older than the flow of human blood in human veins.*
> *My soul has grown deep like the rivers.*
> *I bathed in the Euphrates when dawns were young.*
> *I built my hut near the Congo and it lulled me to sleep.*
> *I looked upon the Nile and raised the pyramids above it.*
> *I heard the singing of the Mississippi when Abe Lincoln went down to New Orleans, and I've seen its muddy bosom turn all golden in the sunset.*
>
> *I've known rivers:*
> *Ancient, dusky rivers.*
> *My soul has grown deep like the rivers.*

My mind locked into Hughes' verse. I knew rivers. It never occurred to me why, but something in me kept my eyes on rivers. When we left home, we crossed an open grate bridge across the old Monongahela River. It was so polluted that it could sustain little life and the few fish found in it could not be eaten. My land was ruined and my river poisoned.

When we passed Lock 4 on the final trip in the move, a river barge piled with bitumen coal bound for the open hearth furnaces was pushing toxins downstream that would soon fall from the sky. It was gold for a few and poison for the rest. The land was sick.

Later the Susquehanna appeared through the bridge barriers with its scattered islands and made me think of my friend, Huckleberry Finn. At nine years of age, he had already marked my life and his story was on a river too. The Delaware, with its massive water and shipping, became a source of fascination as well. It was huge but the real enchantment with it was the story of the landing of my hero, William Penn.

The size of that river gave one pause; the massive amounts of water able to carry ocean bound shipping were amazing, but it was William Penn's first meeting with the natives that held a place in my soul. Penn had a deed from the King of England empowering him to take the land for his colony. Instead of using force, he chose to respect the people who had occupied it for generations and struck a business deal with them that was carried out with integrity. Because of the story of his integrity, the Delaware became a sacred stream of Ganges proportion for me.

We went home often those first years. The Pennsylvania Turnpike took us over the Susquehanna, and when I saw that, it made me feel like we were indeed headed home. And when we crossed it headed back, that's when the loneliness for my land would return because the big city was just over the rise and round a bend.

When traveling home to Donora we'd get off the Turnpike and I'd start to look for the lights of Lock 4 with the town of Charleroi reflected on the Monongahela. The hum of the tires on the open grate bridge sang a welcome song that I can't forget. It was my land and my river. Every morning after a trip from Philadelphia, I would head down the mountain to Eldora to see Aunt Myrtle and to see if the hand painted sign on the gate still said, "Farm for Sale. " It always did and I always dreamed of taking the sign down because the farm was mine – it was my land.

Then one day, Aunt Myrtle did sell the farm and married a kinder man. The farm was forever out of my reach and I was left to travel the road on the opposite ridge and look across the valley at my land. When I made one final trip to see the farm later in life, the barn was felled by neglect and all I could do was to stare in disbelief. My heart hurt and my soul ached. The condition of the barn spoke of contempt for the land.

I can't help but wonder that my spiritual path has been so closely attached to the land and frankly, it never occurred to me that they were connected at all, until after some contemplation my rather imaginative mind composed a story of rivers and land to explain the proliferation of Christian denominations and the amazing similarities between religious ideas all across the world.

I began a fervent search for the authenticity of my religion when I was a kid. I was taught that Evangelical Fundamentalist Christianity was the truth and the only truth produced by the teachings of Jesus Christ. At 14 years of age I began to dispute the claim that salvation by the blood of the crucified Christ changed people. I began to doubt that because I saw some changes but generally, very little evidence that it was true.

I was always pointed toward the Bible as authority and clung to that for most of my life, but the discrepancy between the teachings of the Bible and the behavior of individuals making certain claims as well as the behavior of institutions supporting those claims was enormous. I wanted it to be true. I wanted my beliefs to be substantiated. But the tapestry of this version of God's plan of salvation became frayed and worn thin with the flogging theologians gave it and the thrashing by its followers who wrenched it through the briar patches of twisted behavior.

One obstacle pushed up into my awareness on Easter Sunday morning in my 14th year. I looked out over the congregation of Lehigh Baptist Church from the choir loft. The place was full of people dressed in Easter regalia, and the thought that came to me was, "There has to be more to Christianity than this."

Soon after came the days of Vietnam. I was a miserable failure in Bible College. Northeastern Collegiate Bible Institute was a strict Fundamentalist school and I had too many doubts, questions and the creeping onset of clinical depression. The depression and some apparent disabilities with academics forced me out of the school. The failure in school changed my 4f draft classification to a 1A. Soon the letter came ordering me to report to the Draft board in the early fall of 1966. I avoided the draft by enlisting in the United States Marine Corps.

The Marine Corps is expert at recreating young people into highly disciplined warriors. The screaming, ratcheting orders from Drill Instructors, night time sudden awakenings, bunks tossed, calisthenics, even beatings became a deranged way of life at Parris Island. [The Corps denies the beatings but I was beaten by drill instructors three separate times.] We were in an eight week cycle at the time because Marines were dying hand over fist in Vietnam. The Corps was required to teach 12 weeks' worth of training in less time which meant more intense work at a faster rate. In the last phase of that cycle, things became more ordered and there was a smoother system because they had succeeded in reordering our way of thinking.

Boot Camp at Parris Island was the most difficult thing I had done in my entire life. It changed me and I wouldn't trade it for anything except for one problem: The Corps taught me the value of killing. Even years later when I became a law enforcement officer, it was easy for me to step into the responsibility of being sanctioned to take life with lethal force. I just knew I would do it, as much as I also knew I would not relish it. If it had to be done – I would kill.

I volunteered for Vietnam but the Marine Corps decided that my repeated sinus infections and pneumonia was not what they wanted in a combat Marine. I was given an honorable discharge. I rode the train into Philadelphia in 1967 and emptied my sea bag for the last time. Eventually, I became a Deputy Sheriff in Avery County, North Carolina and eventually settled on specializing in detention. My career lasted seventeen and a half years with the majority of it in the Forsyth County Sheriff's Department as a Jail Operations Sergeant.

In November of 1979 long before I was promoted to sergeant, the Ku Klux Klan and the American Nazi Party massacred five people at a rally in Greensboro, NC. Several of the defendants were housed in our jail and at some point one of the Klansmen complained of chest pain. We were going to have to transport him to the hospital. Captain Wood told Sergeant Murphey to send me with the Klansman in the ambulance.

I picked up my pistol from the control room and went out onto the street. I was looking in parked cars and scanning the rooflines when I heard Captain Wood's voice behind me. "What are you doing Bradstock?"

"Just checking things out to be sure this isn't an escape attempt," I said.

The Captain asked, "What if it is?"

As I looked over the interior of another parked car I replied, "Well Captain, I guess I'll kill him."

I turned to look at him as he said, "Well, if you won't, I'll go."

Without a second thought, without a bit of fear or speck of drama, I just said, "Not a problem." The Captain turned and went inside.

On the way to the hospital in that rough riding ambulance, a car started tailgating and I began to get nervous. We hit a pothole, the gurney slammed loudly down from a recline to a flat position – and my 38 was in my hand and in the Klansman's face before anybody could blink.

The paramedic shouted, "Whoa, Deputy, that was just the gurney, calm down!" I looked steadily at the Klansman over the barrel of that Smith & Wesson, then at the paramedic, stepped back to look out the back door of the ambulance. There was no longer a car there. I holstered my piece and sat down. The other two started to breathe again and my heart restarted.

In terms of my spiritual life, it's significant that this instinctual reaction was nothing but the sheer power of Marine Corps discipline. There was nothing spiritual or grounded in religion that brought me to the point of flicking my index finger and putting a bullet through a Klansman's head. If I had, it would have altered many lives, but there were no gods or spirits whispering in my ear. From then on, that Klansman's gaze each time he looked at me, spoke of the reality of that dark hole he stared into at the end of my pistol. He knew how close we came to hard reality in that instant. No theology can possible speak louder than that. Only the dream of magical thinking adds in the intervention of a god's will.

One Sunday at Parris Island, the drill instructors marched us to chapel. The chapel was full of recruits and a chaplain held a general, catch-all service. It was innocuous but the stained glass caught my eye. Each window in the chapel had a Biblical theme, with all the characters portrayed in military uniforms. Even Jesus was pictured in battle dress.

I stared at those stained glass scenes with fascination. I'd never noticed how the Bible stories could be adapted to fit a certain point of view before. It was not only a new idea but the process it revealed was mind bending. It's still vivid in my mind.

In the years after that, I had experience after experience with people and Christian leaders who did that very thing: saw their perspective as the only way to view Biblical concepts. The longer I lived, the more I saw, and the more I saw, the more I recognized manipulated scripture and ultimately manipulated truth.

Eventually for me, religion became utterly unreliable. Not only had the Corps changed me into a man with a warrior mindset but a man with a soul prepared for religious wariness. It took several years, but I slid further and further away from my conversion experience as a child.

After my discharge, Dottie and I were married. I attempted another round of Bible College at Philadelphia College of the Bible. My problems with academics continued to stand in my way and I gave up after two semesters of poor grades. Dottie and I took an offer to help build a Christian Camp in North Carolina. But things were not good in that place. My experience and opinion of Christian leadership kept slipping with every year until 1975 when Dottie and I moved to Winston-Salem, NC and I was hired by the Forsyth County Sheriff.

The job change didn't change the downhill turn of my experience with religion. Dottie and I had hard times with our adopted son being diagnosed with a mental illness and our newborn at the edge of life with a rare genetic disease. Spiritual care for us was absent; our pastors were inattentive. We coped on the remaining strength of our own faith.

Meanwhile, the Forsyth County Jail was among the largest in the state and we handled dangerous men without weapons. I thought it wise to get some training to ease my concerns about those dangerous conditions. A poorly written sign on a board nailed over the door announcing a Karate School on a dilapidated building in King, NC attracted me. The teacher, Sheldon, was a slightly built man with long black hair and beard framing the most intense ice blue eyes I'd ever seen. When people met him, they almost always said that he scared them. When I'd ask why, the explanation was always; "His eyes!" Sheldon had a New England accent lisped through jaggy black and broken teeth. He often made an effort to hide them with his lips but tended to let it go after a bit. I liked him.

I spent over ten years studying with Sheldon. He was a true martial artist. His concern was in teaching the art and not simply the American adaptation of fighting techniques attached to a rainbow of colored belts. Too many Americans are obsessed with symbols of advancement, thus the rainbow. Sheldon's system was traditional and deemphasized belt ranking and increased the art. That necessarily includes a certain mindset.

In the traditional Oriental martial arts the art is based on Buddhism and Taoism. I was compelled to study them both and for a long time, though doing so made me feel like a like a heretic. My upbringing in Fundamentalist Evangelical Christianity haunted me in this divergence from strict Bible centered reading. As time went on it became apparent that there was as much, if not more peace taught in those systems than in Christianity, although the message of Jesus Christ was still there for the picking. The old block thrown up in my 14th Easter epiphany kept showing up. And through this persistent excavation, I became more and more certain that there was indeed more to Christianity than was being taught or, for that matter being practiced.

As a part of my martial arts studies over a period of about twelve years, I worked on the practice of meditation. Sheldon integrated meditation in our martial art studies. He taught the benefit of the skill for life in general and in the framework of confronting violence. Meditation is the practice of deep mental focus. A martial arts student who has practiced meditation is more able to concentrate on the moment and use techniques appropriate for the violence he encounters. It conserves strength and maintains body/mind harmony in a way that allays self-destructive fear and anger. I also studied for a brief time with a Kung Fu master and a Hindu couple who taught a different style of meditation. Their names slip my mind but their teachings remain.

I found myself exploring the Tao, the Buddha, the Desert Fathers and because of the abuse by Christian teachers and leaders in my own experience in Bible College and church, I drifted away from Evangelical Bible based Christianity and began appreciating my faith outside denominational stockades.

During that time I discovered the Quaker writer, Richard Foster. I was surprised because I thought that Quakerism was history. My childhood hero was William Penn and I had stood at the feet of his statue in Philadelphia. Dad worked for the city and got certain doors unlocked so that we could stand at the base on top of city hall. I was awed by the statue. Penn was a hero in my mind and so the massive statue was equal to the vision of a kid's ideals. Because of the discovery of Foster's books I became a Quaker. Foster taught in his book, *A Celebration of Discipline*, the very things I was looking for in Christianity. My eager mind went after Quakerism thinking it was finally the solution that would rid me of this unyielding blockade in my soul that was now decades old.

Unfortunately, I was wrong again. While more organic, the faith turned out to be more about tradition and rhetoric than the earthy teachings of Jesus. Fortunately, I never gave up on my study of Oriental wisdom. I began to discover that Oriental thought actually enhanced my Christian faith system. The teachings of Jesus seemed so close to Lao Tsu and Buddha that I wondered what Christianity would look like if it had originated in the Far East rather than in the Middle East.

That begged a question. Does religion emerge from culture? What if there is a particular truth and it is found almost everywhere in the world but is stated and acted upon differently depending on the culture? What would be the source of that truth? I can't say that I came up with it on my own because I'd been reading a lot of Matthew Fox's rendering of Meister Eckhart. There's a book in my library by Matthew Fox entitled, *One River Many Wells* (Fox, 2000). He quotes Eckhart:

> *"Divinity is an underground river that no one can stop and no one can dam up."*

Several decades ago, we needed our real well cleaned out and called a well company. The old man who had started the company came on our job. They went through some procedures and pumped the well dry. Then he allowed the well to start refilling. He lifted a large round mirror above the well and focused the reflected light into the bottom of the well and asked me to come over to him. He said, "Look. Do you see the water coming into the bottom of the well? The Earth is like the body. It has arteries, veins and capillaries. Look there. See the very strong stream bubbling up? It's a vein. The two little ones are capillaries. You have a good well."

Somewhere along the line I put the idea of divinity as an underground river together with the streams the old man showed me in my well. I envisioned religion as involving both wells and springs. Some spirit wells are artesian, and some just ordinary wells. I also imagined some of the spirit outlets as springs leaking water out of the spirit source. The supplier of these spirit outlets would be the divine, and the outlets themselves not religions but individuals. The individual sources might be strongly tied to groups, but some might arise as more independent individuals. The flow of the Spirit would carve its way through the landscape in which it arose. The land and the stream shape each other; a mutual carving and crafting based on the complexities of the Earth's spiritual/geological history. The Spirit and the cultural land through which it flows determines the shape the religion takes.

If Jesus had traveled to India during the years absent from his history and decided to remain there rather than return to the chaos in Roman occupied Israel, what would the religion named after him look like? Would it have been less true? Would he no longer have been the only son of the one and only God? Would Christianity have been influenced by Hinduism which was already well developed? The only thing I could determine from these musings was that Christianity would have indeed looked differently due to the culture in which it rose and flowed to its destination.

Culture is also shaped by the land. Not an allegorical land but the actual land – the earth. The physical environment itself is shaped by the earth. It is ultimately the land that determines how a group of people hunt and plant and what it is they hunt for or what can be harvested from the land. The soil and its chemical makeup make all the difference to every living thing.

Part of my grief for the loss of my land was that I was then thrown into the middle of an urban place that was not poisoned by the emissions of steel mills but defaced by asphalt and crowding. The land was constantly being coated and sterilized by concrete slabs with asphalt icing that permitted no life at all. I adapted as all healthy human beings do, but I don't see adaptability as rationalization for killing the land no more than I could have rationalized the killing of another human being. I lived with it because I was forced to do so.

This imaginative spiritual project gave me a cerebral pathway to connect the rivers I knew to the flow of the Spirit through the landscape of my life. It shaped me and I shaped it. I was fashioned to question and was often seen as defiant by Evangelical pastors, lay fundamentalist Christians over the years. But I didn't ask questions to be defiant; I asked because I longed for answers. Thinking in terms of land, when I asked questions, I tended to wash soil away from rock. It seems that those who desperately wanted the contours of their religious terrain to remain unchallenged resented me and my manner. For them I was like the process that shaped the Monongahela River. Wikipedia (Wikipedia) states:

> The Native American word *Monongahela* means "falling banks", in reference to the geological instability of the river's banks. Moravian missionary David Zeisberger (1721–1808) gave this account of the naming: "In the Indian tongue the name of this river was Mechmenawungihilla (alternatively spelled Menawngihella), which signifies a high bank, which is ever washed out and therefore collapses."[11]

This is the work of the river, to carve its bed and to take the land new places and to greater width or depth, without killing it. Religious canyon carvers are disliked and often marginalized or worse. They are safer located on the peripheries where they can be scotched with sea walls and berms made of dogma and tradition fashioned to suit the builders.

In the book, *God is Red* (Deloria, 2003), I discovered something that helped me further understand why I seemed to sense my spirit's tie to the land. He says:

> If we recall the thrust of Jewish history and its eschatology in the time of Jesus, we come to recognize that land, the promised land, has remained as a constant and tangible element of religious experiences of societies.

This came as a flash of insight for me as it affirmed that the entire history of the Jewish people was indeed about land! I was stunned when I read on further in the text,

> ...by substituting heaven for the tangible restoration of Palestine to the Jews by driving the Romans out, Christians eliminated the dimension of land from religion...

As I studied this material, I suddenly looked up from the page and thought, "Of course I feel a kinship to the land and the rivers. Religion arises out of the land."

There were other factors, but this was the final piece to fall in place. The enormous work by systematic Christianity to wrench itself from the land left me and perhaps others lonely for a major piece that was missing. We are seeing some of that return with certain Christian groups acquiescing to the needs of a battered environment.

I recall a poem I once wrote which is now lost. It was entitled, "I Know This One." It was inspired by two major passages in the New Testament. The first was in chapter one of the Gospel of John, where the apostle makes the claim that Jesus Christ is the Word and the Light:

All things were made by him and without him was not anything made that was made. (JOHN 1:3 KJV)

Then John restates it for emphasis in verse 10:

He was in the world and the world was made by him...

That identifies Christ as the creative force for all things in the world. It leaves nothing out. It excludes nothing including the land and the living things it produces. The second passage confirmed this connection for me as I considered the direction my mind was taking. The 27th chapter of Matthew describes the crucifixion of Jesus. Matthew then lists the natural events that occurred upon the death and dying of Christ. He says that darkness covered the land and at his time of death, the earth quaked.

My lost poem connected Christ with the land, starting with his blood seeping into the roughhewn wood of the cross that says, "I know this one." It speaks to the earth and the Earth says, "I know this one."

My poem went across the spectrum of living things who realize as did the centurion, that this was their very creator. The poem spoke in writing what my soul had been sensing much of my life: the spirit and its religion evolves out of the land. To rip the spirit out of the land and give it to an imaginary intangible place above the clouds is to tear out the "more" of Christianity. What's left is soulless and open to hypocrisy, institutional control, manipulative games and cheap cliché. Without a connection to the land, there is only theory; and eventually, I concluded that all doctrine is unsubstantiated, improbable theory; much of it just sanctified magic.

Quakerism seemed to be the logical place for me long before I discovered this affirmation of my religious need for the land. There was something earthy and relevant to humanity within Quakerism. It seemed to be a system that had a grasp of the earth by minimizing the constant prattle about heaven and the dangers of hell. The abstract salvation of souls seemed absurd in the light of easing the suffering of concrete human beings, and I was pulled into that wholeheartedly. There was the promise of simplicity. The conspicuous consumerism running rampant in the massive building of family life centers and mega churches is a symptom of the lack of simplicity and care for the needs of individuals. Quakers made a historical and systemic claim of reaching out to the weak and helpless.

In the little book, *Peace Prayers* (Bradbury, 1992), a short poem became a touchstone for me.

> *For the Quakers*
> *Theirs is the gentle finger on the pulse,*
> *Of war's old woe.*
> *Persistent, with clear unrancored eyes,*
> *Of faith they go,*
> *Where disillusionment lost the charted way.*
> *Unerringly,*
> *They reach across the desperate long miles,*
> *The sullen sea,*
> *And find the thin small fingers in the cold,*
> *And touch and hold.*

But regrettably, my idealism about the historical Society of Friends and the religious descendants of William Penn was soon deflated. I had made yet another mistake in believing what I read.

Within a few months of joining the Quakers in the early 1990's at a local Friend's meeting, I ran headlong into the rancor that this little poem promised was absent from the Society of Friends. I experienced foolish spending on structures, lying from the pastorate and bloodletting about theology. I observed meanness and hostility across the membership of the association we joined, North Carolina Yearly Meeting (FUM). The jaw-dropping ugliness displayed repeatedly in that organization was over several things, but since the 1990's the rancor settled in on homosexuality.

Yet it wasn't merely about homosexuality itself, it was also about scriptural interpretation. The majority of meetings in NCYM (FUM) became embroiled over differences about the authority of the scriptures, the atonement and the definition of a "real Quaker" or a "real Christian." The effort of the Yearly Meeting was no longer to *find the thin small fingers in the cold, And touch and hold*. The focus of factions within the Yearly Meeting was to score points against each other in theology and its theories about the condition of human beings. The tradition of peace and tolerance was being lifted into heavenly heights of theological theory. The Quakers of NCYM (FUM) had ignition and had lift-off. They left the earth.

The behavior of NCYM(FUM) became mean and dysfunctional. One pastor related to me that several other pastors began sending him threatening and harassing mail. It so happened that this pastor was strongly advocating for Gays and Lesbians. He told me that he called the Postal Inspector and was told that the letters were indeed in violation of Federal Law. Since the Inspector's office had bigger fish to fry and didn't have the resources to work on the case, the pastor hired a private investigator and between him and the P. I., they found the authors of the letters; all pastors in NCYM(FUM). When he confronted them, they begged him not to expose them.

He was satisfied. I was not. It angered me and the ideals that I sought in The Religious Society of Friends seemed to be only on paper and the organic, earthy reaching out to the suffering was drowning in the same airy-fairy battles over dogmatic theories.

Shamefully, these battles were not handled as intelligent quarrels over ideas. By the middle of this decade the Evangelical, Fundamentalist meetings became cruel, and NCYM (FUM) Leaders seemed to allow the abusive behavior.

I was also amazed that the older, larger meetings of a more tolerant mind just drifted along as if none of the misbehavior of Yearly Meeting mattered. They seemed to be on another planet or at least comfortably untouched by the bloody skirmishes beneath them.

This was a stance that passively enabled the abuse. I had come to the end of my tolerance for the cruelty and was on the verge of leaving Quakerism altogether, when we discovered a small meeting just off of the Blue Ridge Parkway in Virginia. They were amazing people; that group of 12 were open to gay men and had the habit of giving their money away every month. There was a pastor name Tony Lowe, but he refused a salary and we met with them in Tony and Judy's home.

There were problems of course. But the problems were worked out with reason and love. After one visit to Fancy Gap Friends, Dottie and I were headed south on US 52 to go home and I declared, "God, I love these people!"

We joined the meeting. But it had become a pariah in its larger association, Surry Quarterly Meeting, part of North Carolina Yearly Meeting. Tony and Judy attended a Quarterly meeting and it turned dark and mean. Because Fancy Gap's clerk at the time was gay, members of Surry Quarter began calling us out. It was ugly; we were condemned to hell, rebuked as tools of Satan and personally attacked verbally. Tony's recall of the 2 hours they endured that barrage of cruelty had me listening with my mouth hanging open.

The meeting debated for some time about the value of speaking truth to power and being a presence of peace in that situation. Eventually though, Fancy Gap Friends determined that association with NCYM (FUM) and Surry Quarterly Meeting was draining our energy and we needed to extract ourselves from the abusive system. My question as the clerk of monthly meeting was, "Since when does the Society of Friends tolerate abusive and cruel behavior?" We posed that to Yearly Meeting Executive Committee with our letter of resignation. The letter was finally acknowledged about a year or so later after its disregard was pointed out.

Eventually, it came to me that I was hanging on to an abusive system that behaved much like the population of the jail that I worked in. Pastors had turned to crime and were guilty of breaking postal regulations, Quakers were name calling and threatening with a vehemence that bordered on physical violence but never actually stepped over that line.

I was finished. The Cosmic Christ that Matthew Fox spoke of in his book by that name was nowhere near the Society of Friends as far as I had experienced. Not only was I finished with the Quakerism that I had experienced, I became suspicious of the rest of it.

This was the point at which I had to review my entire experience with Christianity. In fact, I began an honest search of all of my beliefs. Over the years between working in law enforcement and moving forward in this search, I had traveled slowly through college, struggling for years to work and study until I finally finished with a doctorate in Pastoral Counseling. That led to a job offer at Hospice and Palliative Care in Winston-Salem, N. C. as a chaplain.

Hospice chaplains work with people of all religions and denominations with the goal of helping the patient and family find comfort in their own religion. Every day, I worked with many different kinds of Christianity and sometimes other religions and even atheists. I was both enlightened and comforted knowing that most belief systems I encountered offered hope and comfort. That work lasted a little more than a decade and gradually taught me to be fair and objective in my consideration of my life in Christianity.

Unfortunately, God himself came up short in my review. The more I studied the further I moved toward questioning the reality of this super-being I had followed all of my life. Yet I moved toward Deism rather than Atheism, because I just couldn't abandon my life-long belief in God. But Deism was also unsatisfactory in that instead of a contentious God who demanded bloodshed and slaughter, the deist God just created, shrugged his shoulders and walked off.

From there, I just didn't know what to believe; rocking back and forth between faith and fact. Agnosticism held a place in my spiritual life for a small period of time but I felt adrift with anger pulling me one way and the habit of identity with religion the other. Finally, Atheism became a safe harbor from the vitriol and venom of religion. But that meant to renounce the mystery of the earth and the rivers, and I was not whole-heartily an Atheist.

Buddhism began drifting my way again and the books came back off of my shelves and out of the stacks. That marked the end of the life-long journey as a Christian. I was now part of a distinct sector of the American population, what one author has called, a "Done." He described it as a new cohort out of American Christianity.

On December 20th, 2015, I took my vows as a student of Buddhism. There were seven of us in the little retreat house in Piedmont, North Carolina, and my new teacher was dressed in his brown and black Zen robes. We began a short period of meditation and then Bushi said I could begin the vows. After each one, He struck a brass bowl that rang like a gong.

It only took one strike for me to understand the sense of allowing the music to fade before reciting the next vow. It became a sacred process for me: the vow, the gong, the silence and then the next vow. Here are the vows:

> *However innumerable sentient beings are,*
>   *I vow to save them all.*
> *However inexhaustible defilements are,*
>   *I vow to sever them all.*
> *However immeasurable the Dharma-gates* (windows to the essential quality of the self) *are,*
>   *I vow to learn them all.*
> *However unsurpassable the Awakened Way is,*
>   *I vow to achieve it.*

There are just as many problems in Buddhism as in Christianity but they are not my problems. My vows lead me far away from them and the very first vow spiked the practice of the Middle Way right to the earth. I cannot practice Buddhism with integrity without working to ease the suffering of any living thing.

The vows brought my spiritual practice out of the sky. The earth its self is alive and I have made a public commitment to care for it.

The vows also proclaim something that Christianity denies as a system: it is impossible to fulfill these vows. It is admittedly a paradox that draws the truth of living in a universe of paradox and points to the paradox of right living. Christianity rarely admits to its followers that it is impossible to be Christ like. Instead when trouble comes, fingers are pointed, churches split and the Kingdom of Christ is crippled by what Christmas Humphreys (Humphries, 1974) calls, "flogging doctrine to a standstill."

I looked up Quaker Buddhists and discovered that some parts of Quakerism recognized astounding similarities with the Middle Way. When I announced that I'd taken those vows in Meeting for Business, the members of Fancy Gap Friends Meeting took it in stride and I continued as the clerk of Monthly Meeting. One member was only concerned that I might leave the meeting. That was all. That was totality of questions from Friends in that meeting.

The move to Buddhism while tethered to Quakerism is comfortable, allowing me to relearn to love the Society of Friends and return to my love of the land. I still miss my mountain farm with its history, but there is a river here in the Northwestern Piedmont of North Carolina that I've come to enjoy. The Yadkin River is tiny compared to the Delaware, Susquehanna and the Monongahela, but its flow refreshes two states with its wanderings to the Atlantic. I cross it often and ponder its muddy waters.

Several years ago, I was the hospice chaplain for a man who had grown up with the Yadkin River. I coaxed him to tell the stories he had about how the river fed them with fish, game, herbs and wild greens. They were the descendants of poor settlers who remained content with their lives on the land with farming and the Yadkin. I also discovered the old weirs which are stone Vs that the Saura Indians built to catch fish. They still catch an unsuspecting canoeist by sucking him sideways into a line of stones meant to guide fish into hand held baskets over 200 years ago. I love the Yadkin too. It's a part of my life here in North Carolina and fortunately for me, I get to include it in my spiritual practice along with the Carolina red soil.

Once again, my spirit is planted in the land.

Works Cited

Bradbury, B. (1992). *For The Quakers*. (C. Ledingham, Ed.) New York, New York: Harper San Fancisco.

Deloria, V. (2003). *God is Red*. New York: The Putnam Group.

Fox, M. (2000). *One River, Many wells*. New York: Penguin Putnam Inc.

Holy Bible, King James Version. (1967). New York: Oxford University Press.

Hughes, L. (1994). *The Negro Speaks of Rivers*. (A. Rampersand, Ed.) New York, New York, USA: Vintage.

Humphries, C. (1974). Exploring Buddhism. Wheaton, Illinois: The Theosophical Publishing House.

Wikipedia. (n. d.). Retrieved February 2, 2016, from https://en.wikipedia.org/wiki/Monongahela_River

Whittaker Chambers, Alger Hiss, and Quaker Leadership:

A Problem for Friends

H. Larry Ingle

Lately, I have come to see Whittaker Chambers as one of the most fascinating Quakers in the middle of the 20th century. He was also the member of the American Communist Party for about thirteen years, from 1925 to 1938. He joined the rural Pipe Creek Meeting, a part of the Hicksite Baltimore Yearly Meeting in 1943. ("Hicksites" was the nickname for the separatists, known as "tolerants" or "liberals," who divided from the "Orthodox" in 1827 and 1828.) (1) The fact that he is virtually unknown as a Friend to most moderns, including Quakers, however, will serve to illustrate my problem. Why is he so unknown? That is the central question I want to address.

If one ponders that question, it will soon be clear that a person is unknown or forgotten either because she did little of note or because memory of her was glossed over, ignored, even suppressed, by others. There is one more important point that should be made and made strongly and firmly: Chambers turned out to have been right in the matter that brought him to public attention in the first place–his 1948 testimony against another Communist and State Department official, Alger Hiss, who spied for the Soviet Union in the 1930s–and those who long defended Hiss, including Friends, were wrong. This outcome is certainly noteworthy, but it too is little noted.

Whittaker Chambers, who lived from 1901 to 1961, certainly did something and certainly created waves that still ripple. Never graduating from college, he was a dumpy looking fellow, dressed in wrinkled, rumpled suits; he swallowed his words, seemed to have no sense of humor, and was certainly not very outgoing. A talented writer, however, he was employed as a writer-editor by *Time* Magazine in its 1940s heyday.

This unprepossessing person came to public notice when he testified before the House Committee on Un-American Activities Committee on August 3, 1948, that a prominent State Department bureaucrat in the 1930s, Alger Hiss, graduate of the John Hopkins University and Harvard Law School, was a Communist who purloined documents from the State Department; he passed them along to Chambers, the Friend testified, who took them to New York, where they were sent on to Moscow. It was not illegal in 1948 to be a Communist, and the statute of limitations had expired on espionage, so Hiss could not be prosecuted for the activities that Chambers testified about. But as 1948 was a presidential election year, Chambers's testimony was politically explosive for the Democratic Truman administration. So in 1949, it charged Hiss with lying under oath when he denied giving Chambers unauthorized documents. Tried in federal court in New York, his trial ended in a hung jury, whereupon he faced a second trial and another jury under a different judge, was convicted of perjury on January 21, 1950, and sentenced to five years in federal prison. Chambers's testimony had been legally validated even if it proved to be politically and explosively challenged. (2)

Two years later, Chambers published a better than 800-page memoir, *Witness*, that quickly became a classic bestseller and a brilliant work of its genre; it was, and is, compelling reading indeed. Quakers might well place it on the same shelf right beside other journals from their fellow believers from the 17th, 18th, and 19th centuries, one of the few from the last hundred years. In *Witness*, Chambers carried on a dialogue with experience in a way that revealed how God had dealt with him, as his life twisted and turned through and around the obstacles he faced. In his book, Chambers's mystical religious faith, expressed outwardly in Quakerism, explained to his satisfaction what he believed lay at the base of his life. As a Quaker journal, it probably sold more copies than any of the others, with the possible exception of Friends principal founder George Fox's *Journal*, which of course had more than a 250-year headstart on his. (3)

Observers at the time and later might have thought that Quakers would have gushed over the book and taken it and its author to heart. Chambers's testimonial to his Quakerism was as convincing to a reader as his statements about Hiss's perjury at the second jury trial. On page five of his Introduction, which he entitled "Letter to My Children," he asserted that "I was a witness," not "a witness *against* something" but "a witness for something": "a man whose life and faith are so completely one that when the challenge comes to step out and testify for his faith, he does so, disregarding all risks, accepting all consequences." If that is not a telling, succinct statement of the essence of Quakerism, I have never seen one. (4) Reading it, I think immediately of the query still used among Friends in Southern Appalachian Yearly Meeting and Association, "Do all aspects of your life bear the same witness?"

Chambers did not come to Friends because of their social testimonies, no matter how important they might be. "I was not seeking ethics," he stated, "I was seeking God." In fact, he held back in asking for membership because he was afraid that his inability to embrace pacifism fully would be a strike against him when he applied; as a fierce anti-Communist, he believed Communism was so monstrously evil that it would conceivably have to be resisted by force. This stance would "forever bar . . . me from the peace within which it was my pathos to crave, but not my right to share." Earlier in his search, believing himself closed off from Friends, he listened to two Episcopal friends who convinced him in 1940 to go to vespers at the unfinished Cathedral of St. John the Divine in New York. He was confirmed and baptized in that church on September 26, 1940, about a year and a half after he had taken a job as a book reviewer at *Time* magazine. (5)

Chambers found the service at the altar to be solemn, but the little group, mostly older folk, he worshipped with at night "seemed less like the bearers of those glad tidings that had once stirred and transformed men's souls than survivors of a spiritual catastrophe." What he was looking for, clearly, was what that second generation William Penn called "Primitive Christianity Revived" and a place he could encounter God's spirit silence: "the silence of Quaker worship continued to reach out and draw me irresistibly to it." It is not clear why he sensed this drawing, for he had never attended a meeting of Friends. His father's mother, his grandmother, had told him stories about the rural Quaker meeting in Pennsylvania that she had attended after the Civil War, but he had never been to one. And his Chambers surname dotted Quaker history. At this point, still formally an Episcopalian, he picked up Quaker founder George Fox's *Journal*, the first Quaker book he had ever opened.

It immediately spoke to his condition. "It summoned me," he wrote, "to know the Inward Light, that of God within myself, as within all other men without exception." It called him to "a simplicity of spirit whose first commandment is compassion." And as to his qualms about pacifism, he realized that the same spirit, "if it truly stirs, never brings peace, but always brings a sword." He knew Fox "as if we had spoken face to face." He was "a man of force," a man of the people, whether they were herding sheep, suffering doggedly, or in stinking prisons, experiencing bloody beatings.

So Chambers betook himself to a Wednesday evening meeting at the Orthodox 20th Street Meetinghouse in Manhattan, one led by the charismatic Arthur Burke. All we know about the time was that it was after he was confirmed into the Episcopal Church but before he joined Friends. These meetings were among, he testified, the "decisive experiences of my life." Occasionally the worshippers and God's present spirit made the meetings so alive that they seemed to ebb and flow with great pulsations, throbbing with palpable transcendent life. Once Burke explained, in words that Chambers probably failed to recognize as traditional Quaker language, "This meeting has had a divine covering." He quoted Scottish Friend Robert Barclay, that when he felt this secret power "I gave way unto it, [and] I found the evil weakening in me and the good raised up." After such unified collective experiences, Chambers told himself and recorded in his memoir, "I was in fact, though not yet in name, a Quaker."

He only had to find a way to seal this convincement. That was not difficult. The Chambers family lived on a farm near Westminster, Maryland, and about a dozen miles away, near Union Bridge, was a small Hicksite Friends meeting called Pipe Creek, where he and his nearly nine-year old daughter drove one summer Sunday morning. The meeting place stood on top of slight rise, surrounded by bushes and trees with a graveyard behind.

The meeting was small, probably about six or so Friends, and silent that morning. The longest spider web they had ever seen looped from wall to wall, and they watched it swaying in the slight breeze that came in through the two open doors and windows. Father Chambers, at least, learned that morning the meaning of the 17th century Quaker phrase, "in the silence of the creature" and gave thanks to God that he had come home. On the way home, he asked Ellen what she had done during the silence, and she said that she had watched the spider web drift in the air; she wanted to know what they others were doing, and her father said they were listening for the voice of God. Did they hear it, she wanted to know? He thought for a moment, perhaps remembering the galvanizing experiences he had had at 20th Street meeting, and replied, "No, I am afraid not that time." (6)

The family of four, Whittaker, Esther, Ellen, and son John, asked to join the meeting and were admitted on August 17, 1943. They were presently taking an active role in the small group, over the next five years one or all appointed to be representatives to the regional quarterly meeting. (7) For Chambers himself, the meeting and his membership with it were primary, judging from the attention he gave it in *Witness*; there he reiterated its appeal. When he sought to document how close the Hisses and the Chamberses were in the 1930s, he instanced the fact that both appreciated "the simplicity inherent in the Quaker way of life" and "the rejection of the pursuit of pleasure as an end in life." Both families similarly distrusted "materialism in its commonest forms of success and comfort." (Though not a Quaker, Priscilla Hiss had gone to Bryn Mawr College, founded by Orthodox Friends, and she and her husband used the plain language "thee" and "thy" at home when they conversed with each other.)

Chambers believed that turning his back on Communism and embracing capitalism, as he explained dramatically in his memoir, meant "leaving the winning world for the losing world," the world destined for defeat in the world's coming revolutionary conflict. Quakerism offered him a faith that put intrinsic human values above material ones. It was no wonder that he valued simplicity so much–it formed the basis of his world. He told a secular friend that when he joined the meeting he found "an experience I have been seeking all my life. To sit in silence with my children beside me and our friends about me is perhaps more than I have any right to expect in life. And yet I have always wanted goodness, never evil." (8)

In fact, Chambers emphasized that he had always abhorred war, insisting that he was attracted to Communism back in the 1920s because he believed that it offered a solution to the problem of war. Yet the modern Quakers at Pipe Creek did not require him to abjure all war but gave him the right to determine his stance in any future conflict by examining his conscience. He explored old Quaker writers, such as Rhode Islander Job Scott from the 18th century, who sought to encourage Friends not to forget the old testimonies about apparel, tithing, and language, not in and of themselves, but as ways to bear a silent and living testimony, witnessing to the modern world that what it would "hold dear and indispensable are at the root of its despair."

In this sense the rumpled suit he often wore seemed to symbolize his Quaker plainness and stood as a judgment against superfluity. Before long, he realized that once he had truly been reached by the life of Quakerism, he "felt a completion such a I had never known before–an adulthood, a maturity, that marked off the [previous] forty years of my life as a childhood. . . . I could never be a complete man without God." This new, totally reinvigorated sense of renewal aroused his compassion without being rooted in any kind of smugness or self-righteousness when it came to other people. He was a changed person indeed. (9)

Chambers's convincement and uniting with Friends, as he described them in his memoir, read so convincingly that an outsider or observer looking back now would expect other Quakers to have rushed to embrace and welcome their new fellow believer. How wrong that would be. The Hicksite periodical, *Friends Intelligencer*, which circulated among Friends with whom Pipe Creek Meeting was affiliated, commented in May 1949 on the "alleged membership" of Chambers in a Quaker meeting. Having received queries from its readers regarding Chambers's statement that "being a Quaker, he did not want to hurt anybody," the editor confessed to having no more information than had appeared in the secular press. But in the spirit of inclusiveness, Chambers was a offered a tepid endorsement: "Friends will, we hope, consider him one of theirs in the community of seekers after truth and perfection."

This brief editorial comment was the closest any Friend came to siding publicly with Chambers after his testimony revealing the presence of Communists within the United States government. (10) That the case as it developed would become the touchstone of the conflict between liberals and conservatives in the late 1940s and 1950s and beyond and make Chambers a hero of the right put such Friends squarely on the liberal side politically, a spot they seemed quite content to occupy.

The same magazine all but ignored *Witness* when it appeared in May 1952 but it is possible to glean some assumptions of its editors if we look at it with care. It published a "review" which consisted of a meager seven lines, but was seven more than any other

Quaker periodical printed. Let me present them all so readers can get their flavor directly:

> "This book contains about five times the amount of material recently published in the *Saturday Evening Post*. As is now generally known, the story is a blending of autobiographical and political material. The present volume is likely to intensify the partisanship on both sides already present in many minds. The book contains a number of references to Friends." (11)

Three things seem immediately clear from these four sentences: 1) the editors believed that many readers had already read portions of the book in the *Saturday Evening Post*, 2) the editors assumed that most alert folk among its readers were already aware of the broad outlines of the story, and 3) though containing some references to Quakers, the book was partisanly oriented and likely to intensify that partisanship.

On the other hand, the Hicksite journal could hardly ignore the best-known Quaker in the United States after former President Herbert Hoover. This was Clarence Pickett, the long-time, since 1929, executive secretary of the American Friends Service Committee. AFSC was the most prominent Quaker organization in the country, one that had just, in 1947, received the Nobel Peace Prize in the name of all Quakers from the hand of the Norwegian king. Pickett, born in Illinois but growing up in Kansas among programmed Orthodox Quakers, went to William Penn College in Oskaloosa, Iowa, and then to Harford Theological Seminary in Connecticut. He served as pastor in Toronto and Oskaloosa and then lived in Richmond, Indiana, the home of Five Years Meeting, the umbrella organization for programmed Friends. There he worked for nine years as a Quaker bureaucrat and Earlham College professor.

As AFSC executive, he lived in the Philadelphia area and headed up the group's increasingly multifaceted activities –relief work, both international and domestic, racial relations, peace education, labor unions, housing, and the like–many of them bringing him into close contact with the Roosevelt family in the White House. He and his biographer, Lawrence Miller, liked to stress his friendship with Eleanor Roosevelt, liberal wife of the liberal President. Pickett was clearly a man of broad influence and contacts well beyond the somewhat narrow confines of the Society of Friends. In 1956, a national Quaker publication assessed him "as probably the best known and widely acclaimed leader in the Quaker field at present." In myriad ways when he spoke or acted, many Friends naturally followed his lead. (12)

Pickett was also involved directly in the Chambers-Hiss matter. He knew Hiss, who had served as speaker at AFSC's week-long summer institutes on foreign affairs and, as president of the

Carnegie Endowment for International Peace when Chambers testified about his associations in the 1930s, had evaluated AFSC's peace education work. Though Pickett had never met Chambers, he reached out to him after the testimony. They conferred at the Homewood Friends Meetinghouse in Baltimore, where Pickett tried to convince him to agree to draw up a joint statement with Hiss that could settle the broad issues between them without mutual libel suits.

That effort failed, and Pickett came away convinced that Chambers was a bit unstable. Then at Hiss's second trial for perjury, Pickett, with approval from AFSC's board, offered himself as a character witness for the defendant, a move that must have sent Chambers reeling, for he had, of course, repeated his charges of treachery and espionage for the other side. Hiss's conviction certainly did nothing to warm relations between the two Friends, but Pickett's testimony won warm (but privately expressed) words from the editor of the Orthodox Quaker journal, *The Friend*: "Thee has put thyself on the record of championing justice and true patriotism, which is good for the fame of the A.F.S.C. and the welfare of the country." (13)

Relations between Pickett and Chambers did not improve when *Witness* came out either. Its publisher, Random House, naturally wanted to attract as much attention to the book as possible. They succeeded. Serialized over ten issues of the *Saturday Evening Post*–the cover story for its first installment delayed the usual Norman Rockwell painting, this one of leaping cheerleaders–and the main selection of June's Book of the Month Club, the book immediately corralled public attention. Excerpts were even read over the radio. *Saturday Review*, the nation's premier book review, featured the book on its cover for May 24, with better than a six-page series of reviews from a stellar panel of commentators, with Arthur M. Schlesinger, Jr., probably the nation's foremost liberal intellectual heading it up; Richard Nixon, Senator from California and like Chambers a Quaker, was the only Republican among the five reviewers. Of them, only Schlesinger noted that Chambers had become a Friend, twice, but both times only in passing; Nixon, who might have been expected to comment on his Friend's discovery, referred only to the fact that the author had found a non-specific "counter-faith," but his reference remained so generic that he did not name its meeting place. (14)

Three weeks later a boxed letter to *Saturday Review* from Pickett appeared. Not a review, it was even more fundamental, questioning whether Chambers understood his new faith, Quakerism, theologically. Coming as it did from a Quaker as prestigious and well known as Pickett, it had the effect at least of warning readers that they should not take Chambers's views of Quakerism seriously, and at most suggesting to Friends that he was not, as far as theology was concerned, a real Quaker regardless of his membership. (Such questioning of another's theology, however common in other

Christian groups, was by then rare indeed among Hicksite Friends, particularly those who lived in the east; that a secular magazine carried it, and put it inside a box to draw readers' attention, gives the entire affair a more powerful imprimatur.)

The letter harked back to a March 8, 1948, cover story for *Time* that senior editor Chambers had written, on Union Theological Seminary's Reinhold Niebuhr. The story explored Niebuhr's "neo-orthodoxy," then an increasingly popular and much discussed theology among Protestant Christians. It argued that, contrary to the position taken by liberal Christians, God was not so much immanent in human affairs as separated and totally apart from them. Only when God chose to intervene, by grace, with humans were they able to experience the divine presence; God was totally transcendent and different from human creatures and their relationship was a one-way affair, determined by the divine will, which tended to be inscrutable.

Growing out of Calvinism, this theology represented the kind of thing that the earliest Quakers had reacted strongly against. Moreover, it had clear political dimensions: Niebuhr had once been an active pacifist but broke ranks and became a foreign policy "realist", supporting the U.S. against Germany and Japan in World War II, then afterward backed Cold War anti-communism and even the development of nuclear weapons. Both Niebuhr's politics and his theology were targets of the ire of liberal pacifist Christians like Pickett.

Chambers's attendance at Quaker meetings for worship, Pickett conceded, had brought him "moments of real peace and enlightenment." This was an achievement he applauded. But then, taking on a bit of a hectoring tone, Pickett lectured *Time*'s author that he had followed neo-orthodox thinkers so far that he had not fully understood Quakers. Pickett insisted that Friends found God within themselves, that the Inward Light, the inner voice, was there for them at any time. "For the Quaker, the discovery of God is an inward experience. He is not far from any of us at any time, and the constant and immediate recognition of His presence is the source of both peace and social concern."

In his final comment, Pickett called into question all the positive statements that permeated *Witness* about the meaningfulness of Quakerism to its author: "This all leaves one feeling that religious assurance is yet to come to this troubled spirit, and that the race with catastrophe [for him] is not over." To drive this conclusion home for Friends, within days the Hicksite *Friends Intelligencer*, reprinted the above on its opening page for Friends to ponder when they considered Chambers's experiences with his faith. And a few days later, Senator Nixon passed along the intelligence to Chambers that Pickett had "denounced" him for misrepresenting Quakers.

It is impossible to tell for sure how Pickett and his many Friends reacted to the overall Hiss-Chambers case with its long aftermath, but it does seem significant that neither Chambers nor

Hiss—or for that matter, even Nixon—is mentioned in Pickett's memoir, possibly because Pickett considered it unimportant to the central events of his life or because he hoped people would put it all behind them, as he had evidently tried to do. (15)

Pickett certainly had a valid point about neo-orthodoxy, but his charges in a brief letter to a secular publication went too far; *Saturday Review* was hardly the place to open up and delve into its theological ramifications anyway. Chambers had admitted in *Witness*, "in many ways, the Niebuhr essay [in *Time*] was a statement of my own religious faith at the time." But that did not necessarily negate his and Quakers' experiences, the latter going back over the centuries. One could hold that God chose when to appear to people, whether waiting in silence or not, and still accurately affirm that the observant Friend had experienced God's presence in accordance with Quakers' beliefs. For Pickett to declare that Chambers had drifted from the Quaker position that God's divine spirit, whether referred to as God, Christ, the Spirit, or the Inward Light, could come to worshippers was specious indeed. Chambers's explanation of his encounters with the Christ-Spirit in *Witness* certainly testified that God had and could and had led him in worship, whether as an Episcopalian or a Friend.

Moreover Quakerism had only rarely produced theologians, and Chambers did not lay claim to being one, but he could read and understand Niebuhr—not to mention his own experiences—well enough to know whether the gripping realities he sometimes encountered in silent worship were divine visitations or not. Chambers ended his *Time* essay on Niebuhr by quoting his subject at his unconsciously Quaker best: "You don't get world government by drawing up a fine constitution. You get it through the process of history. You grow into it." In other words, Niebuhr believed one learned from experience. (16) In the same fashion Friends likewise knew that they grew into truth from the experiences they insisted would lead them into all truth.

Chambers spoke little of Friends or his experiences in Quaker meetings after he published his memoir in 1952, permitting that volume to illuminate how God had dealt with him up to that time. But with some sarcasm he could understandably take aim at Pickett and even himself on occasion. In a throwaway line in a letter to a friend, he implicitly criticized himself for using some biting language, remarking "Such language—and from a Quaker too." But he saved his choicest witty dig for Pickett, telling the same friend, "It is recorded that at certain meetings of George Fox, the spiritual intensity was such that the very walls of the meeting vibrated. Now," he concluded, "we have Clarence Pickett." (17) Clearly, Chambers was not always as dour as his suits made him look.

Chambers's biographer, Sam Tanenhaus, with apparent inadequate research in the Quaker sources, asserted that his subject "began to withdraw" from Quakerism after his daughter was denied admission in 1951 to Swarthmore College, an elite Quaker school, but no hard documentary evidence exists to support this claim. To the contrary, he was willing to be publicly identified as a Quaker even in the pages of *National Review*, the outspoken conservative weekly magazine that William F. Buckley, Jr., founded in 1955 to spark a respectable conservative movement in the United States. Even in the brief period in the late 1950s when he was serving as *National Review's* senior editor, he was so described. (18) True, judging from his silence about Quakers after 1952 and the public buffeting he endured from Pickett, he definitely drew back from the Society, but he certainly did not renounce his membership with Pipe Creek, thus remaining a Friend.

There is one more aspect of the impact of the Chambers-Pickett relationship, relatively brief as it was, that needs mentioning and further research. As far as I have been able to glean, Friends left no record that they gave more thought to Chambers after the reviews of *Witness* appeared. The Hicksite weekly, *Friends Intelligencer* published nothing more about Chambers; like Pickett it was silent. So was its successor, *Friends Journal*, which began publishing in 1955. Nixon, an evangelical Friend, remained in contact and occasionally benefited from Chambers's political advice, but their relationship differed markedly from the one either had with Pickett. Nixon, of course, was not part of the Quaker "establishment," certainly not eastern, hardly western.

In Philadelphia, the Mecca of eastern Quakerism, the center of power revolved around Orthodox Friends, who historically took no notice of Hicksites. In 1939 writer Logan Pearsall Smith, who grew up Orthodox, described them as "stratified in social layers of increasing splendor." They exhibited "an immense sense of social superiority" over lesser breeds like Hicksites whom they saw as "outcasts and untouchables and social pariahs." They knew their peers almost by instinct; (19) they did not know Chambers. And with so little attention to him in their Quakerly circles, they had no way to learn of him.

Pickett's negative opinion of Chambers percolated and spread through unprogrammed Quakers, both Orthodox and Hicksites, who by the 1940s were tending toward political liberalism and associating themselves with the Democratic Party. This affinity made them lean pro-Hiss and anti-Chambers. Larry Miller, Pickett's biographer and a weighty Philadelphia Friend himself, publicly reaffirmed as late as 1994 that he shared his subject's view that Hiss was telling the truth in denying Chambers's charges. An academic from Los Angeles, Robert Ellwood, who claimed to be doing research on the Hiss-Chambers matter, wrote nearly 40 years later absolving Friends of any shame they might harbor from associating with Hiss or his wife. And a Friend from New York, George Nicklin confessed in 1995 that he had always believed Hiss was wrongly convicted. (20) From such scattered references, the sense is reinforced that Chambers was one of those "outcasts and pariahs."

Yet–and this complicates the matter of viewing Chambers as some kind of knee-jerk conservative–judging from some of the stands he took on public issues, he was also occasionally willing to be identified with the kind of liberal views that Quakers were championing by this time. (It is not altogether clear when exactly modern Quakers, particularly those in the eastern part of the country, started gravitating toward the "left" side of the political spectrum – almost no research has gone into that question. (21) One major piece of this drift involved a change in the understanding of the peace testimony. Following the Civil War and then World War I, many Friends and yearly meetings quietly shifted from flatly refusing to take part in war because it violated God's law, to emphasizing efforts to prevent war and maintain peace (with actual participation in war left to individual conscience). The creation of the American Friends Service Committee, the Great Depression and advent of the New Deal, and the founding of the Friends Committee on National Legislation, all helped fertilize this change from mid-19th century Whiggery and late 19th and early 20th century Republicanism to Democracy, at least for most eastern and liberal friends.

Chambers, while an easterner and part of a Hicksite meeting, went the other way. He had certainly become a conservative–no doubt about that–but we must not forget that he converted from Communism to Quakerism, not to conservatism. And as we have seen, he did so with his eyes open; he never used the term "Hicksite," as far as we know, but he could hardly have escaped the fact that Pipe Creek Meeting, even, especially, with its members' use of the plain language, was among the group of Friends who had been tagged with "liberal" from their beginning. And, knowing him and his family as members of their community, Pipe Creek Friends came to them, as he said, "at once," when he faced the onslaught of publicity accompanying his testimony against Hiss, the man other Quakers like Pickett viewed as persecuted. (22)

Some of Chambers's political stands during the 1950s would probably have surprised Pickett, but they illustrate that he was a man of complexity and nuance. The most significant was his take on Wisconsin Republican Senator Joseph R. McCarthy. McCarthy, a Roman Catholic, parlayed Chambers's testimony about Hiss into partisan charges that the Democratic Party was the party of traitors who turned a blind eye to the subversion their chosen bureaucrats promoted.

Chambers would have none of this crusade, despite the fact that he was as–or more–anti-Communist than McCarthy. Chambers wrote William F. Buckley, whom he had first met after the latter asked him to write a blurb for a laudatory study of McCarthy that Buckley and his brother-in-law had written, that he considered the Senator a danger to the cause of anti-Communism. "McCarthy will one day," Chambers presciently predicted, "make some irreparable blunder which will play directly into the hands of our common enemy and discredit the whole anti-Communist effort for a long time to come." Two months later, he repeated his warning that McCarthy would likely become a "political godsend" to the Communists because "he scarcely knows what he is doing." (23) These views never became public while Chambers lived, but that detail made them no less telling as evidence of his political acumen.

Or consider Chambers and governmental control over farm crops, something political conservatives could grow apoplectic about without a second thought. In 1954 he wrote two friends about how eight of his Maryland neighbors–one a close friend–were presently going on trial in Baltimore for violating the New Deal's crop controls on growing wheat. Their "position," he summed up, "is preposterous." And he catalogued the reasons why: 1) the country's "farmers have voted for socialization," 2) they did not object to support checks but "to government inspection of their crops," which was part and parcel of subsidies, and 3) they had excess production because modern agriculture just naturally produced massive surpluses. "They voted for a curb on their own incontinent productivity for the same reason that a fat man takes to diet–ultimately to prolong his life." However much he might agree on theoretical grounds with their position, Chambers would not publicly support them. (24)

And then in the pages of *National Review*, he announced that he supported granting a passport for foreign travel to the now-freed Alger Hiss. The State Department under Republican President Dwight Eisenhower considered withholding such carte blanche permission to travel because Hiss was a felon convicted for denying he was a Communist. Why, conservatives yelled, Hiss might use it to go off to Moscow. Chambers doubted that a man who had denied being a Communist for more than a decade would dare show up at the Kremlin. But how could any authentic conservative support restoring his freedom to travel? Well, Chambers responded, as a man of the Right, he had no wish to thereby help "feed the Total State." Besides any American citizen, felon or no, had the right to travel abroad.

Chambers imagined someone muttering, "Why the man is talking like a Liberal." Yet he stood firm, willing, as he said, to draw fire from both sides, "in the No Man's Land between incensed camps." (25)

In September 1954, not long after they first made each other's acquaintance, Chambers told the staunch Roman Catholic Buckley that "I stand within no religious orthodoxy," something that goes a long way in explaining why Quakerism appealed to him. In the same letter, he was equally as blunt about his political creed: "I am not a conservative." He did identify himself as a "man of the Right," because "I mean to uphold capitalism in its American version." But this capitalism, he went on, "is not, and by its essential nature cannot conceivably be, conservative." Trying to create an American conservatism, he concluded, brings its disciples to "a sense of unreality and pessimism on the Right, running off into all manners of crackpotism." (26)

Given these self-characterizations, Chambers could not have surprised *National Review*'s editor when he delivered his text of an assigned review of a new 1957 novel by an author trying to win a favorable audience with conservatives, Ayn Rand. Rand, a Russian émigré whose previous books had celebrated an unabashedly "selfish individualism," was known for flaunting her atheism and disdain for the usual conventionalities–she was often pictured, for example, smoking cigarettes, something proper women avoided in the 1950s. Chambers's review was not quite as colorfully splenetic as one that H.L. Mencken, the notorious cynic of the 1920s, might have turned out, but it was close enough. Entitled "Big Sister Is Watching You," Chambers let loose, his pen dipped in vitriol. He complained about the novel's length at 1168 pages, denied that Rand's favorite philosopher could be Aristotle the Greek but was rather the German thinker Friedrich Nietzsche, and bemoaned her tendency to paint everything and everyone in the darkest blacks and the purest whites.

She was so rigidly theoretical, he said, that her "Randian" man was as materialistic as her crooked "looters." Chambers was especially sarcastic about the last scene in which Rand described a character who made "the Sign of the Dollar" over a "desolate earth." Buckley later claimed that the review had "read Miss Rand right out of the conservative movement." The mail brought in numerous irate dissents. One outraged reader from Columbus, Ohio, pontificated that "Chambers as a Christian Communist is far more dangerous than as a Communist spy." (27)

Such unusual positions for a conservative, a man of the Right, as he preferred to identify himself, illustrate that people who want a total picture have to take care when they look at Chambers–they have to see him as a whole–and they have to see how fundamental his Quakerism was to who he became. For example, the most obvious thing about him at first sight was his crumpled clothing; his suit always seemed as though it needed to be sent to the cleaners for a pressing. The contrast with the trim, well-groomed, almost sleek Hiss was stark. Practically every reporter who saw Chambers remarked on his seeming disregard for his appearance, doubtless ignorant of what he had read in Job Scott, the Rhode Island Quaker of 150 years before, that one should take no regard for his raiment, advice that echoed teacher Jesus in his Sermon on the Mount. Some, like Clarence Pickett, seeing him for the first time, could judge him as perhaps emotionally unstable. His general carriage certainly did not embody the public image that most modern Quakers expected their own to convey.

Such personal considerations were not unimportant, to be sure, but they paled before the central issue, the belief of Hiss's supporters that his innocence and reputation had been destroyed by what they believed were Chambers's lies, probably calculated, perhaps in collaboration with a government witch-hunt. Furthermore, only ten days after Chambers's testimony on August 3,1948, Hiss bestowed credit on his Quaker supporters for staying with him: writing the assistant executive secretary at AFSC, he explained that the "friends have been one of few compensations in this ugly incident." (28) Yet here was Chambers, another Friend, the very cause of "this ugly incident," whose life's future trajectory seldom intersected with the faith that has given his life such meaning.

One might have thought that over the years some Friends would have avidly followed Chambers's post-perjury trial career; the record I found does not inicate that they did. If they had, they might have come to see that he was not some kind of unbending, unthinking, conservative but a man of human complexity and subtlety who took positions that clashed with Quaker testimonies no more than other Friends did. They might have recognized the tragic pain enshrined in both men's careers and even later recognized Chambers for having told the difficult, even shocking truth about Hiss' earlier career, as later events and research confirmed. Some might even have come to celebrate his lonely and stressful witnessing to that truth. And others might have been moved as well to examine, perhaps reject many of their trendy cold war liberal assumptions and, even prejudices.

In such a what-if scenario Chambers would not have distanced himself from the Society of Friends and would have added to their reputation as exemplifying an all-inclusive fellowship of followers of Christ.

As it is, Chambers remains virtually unknown to modern Friends. He is still cloaked in silent obscurity, rather than being remembered as a man who experienced the promptings of God's spirit in their meetings and acted from those leadings to echo the truth he knew. Little more can be asked of a Friend. But more can–and must–be asked of the Society's own leadership, starting in this instance with one as influential as Clarence Pickett, and those who have since trod unknowingly in his footsteps.

Notes

1. On the separation, see H. Larry Ingle, *Quakers in Conflict: The Hicksite Reformation* (Knoxville, Tenn.: University of Tennessee Press, 1986).

2. For the case, see *Allen Weinstein, Perjury: The Hiss-Chambers Case* (New York: Alfred A. Knopf, 1978). On Chambers, see Sam Tanenhaus, *Whittaker Chambers* (New York: Random House, 1997). There is no biography of Hiss, but he produced an unsatisfactory memoir, Alger Hiss, *Recollections of a Life* (New York: Henry Holt & Co., 1988). For a critical look at Hiss, but one which fails also to look at his (or Chambers's) religious faith, see G. Edward White, *Alger Hiss's Looking-Glass Wars: the Covert Life of a Soviet Spy* (New York: Oxford University Press, 2004).

3. Whitaker Chambers, *Witness* (New York: Random House, 1952). On Quaker journals, see Howard H. Brinton, *Quaker Journals: Varieties of Religious Experience among Friends* (Wallingford, Penn.: Pendle Hill Publications, 1972).

4. Chambers, *Witness*, 5.

5. Ibid., 482-83. There is a photocopy documenting Chambers's baptism in Meyer A. Zeligs, *Friendship and Fratricide: An Analysis of Whittaker Chambers and Alger Hiss* (New York: Viking Press, 1967), 328-29.

6. Chambers, *Witness*, 482-85.

7. Pipe Creek Meeting Minutes, Pipe Creek Monthly Meeting Minute Book, 1889-1962, 8 Mo. 17 1943, 266, 270, 271, 276, Friends Historical Library, Swarthmore College, Swarthmore, Penn.

8. Chambers, *Witness*, 25, 362; Richard M. Nixon, *Six Crises* (Garden City, N.Y.: Doubleday & Co. 1962), 23; Chambers to Herbert Solow, 1943, in Weinstein, *Prejury*, 335.

9. Chambers, *Witness*, 193, 288-89.

10. *Friends Intelligencer*, 106 (8 Fifth month, 1949), 15.

11. *Ibid.*, 109 (7 Sixth month 1952), 324.

12. Lawrence Miller, *Witness for Humanity: A Biography of Clarence E. Pickett* (Wallingford, Penn.: Pendle Hill Publications,

1999); Clarence E. Pickett, *For More than Bread: An autobiographical account of twenty-two years' work with the American Friends Service Committee* (Boston: Little, Brown and Co., 1953); Jane P. Rushmore, "We Are Growing Together," *Friends Journal*, 2 (26 May 1956), 327.

13. H. Larry Ingle, *Nixon's First Cover-up: The Religious Life of a Quaker President* (Columbia: University of Missouri Press, 2015), ch. 4; Clarence Pickett to Claude B. Cross, 10, 23 Nov 1949, Richard R. Wood to Pickett, 14 Dec 1949, Gen'l Admn: Individuals, 1949: A. Hiss, AFSC Archives, Philadelphia; United States of America *vs.* Alger Hiss, U.S. District Court, Southern District of New York, court reporters, 13 Dec 1949, 1857-59.

14. Tanenhaus, *Chambers*, 461-62; "Whittaker Chambers and his 'Witness,'" *Saturday Review*, 35 (24 May 1952), 8-14.

15. *Saturday Review*, 35 (14 Jun 52), 32; Chambers, *Witness*, 505-07; the *Time* article can be found in Terry Teachout, ed., *Ghosts on the Roof: Selected Journalism of Whitaker Chambers, 1931-1959* (Washington, D.C.: Regnery Co., 1989), 84-93; Ralph de Toledano, ed., *Notes from the Underground: The Whittaker Chambers-Ralph de Toledano Letters, 1949-1960* (Washington, D.C.: Regnery Publishing, 1997), 85-87; *Friends Intelligencer*, 109 (26 Sixth Month 1952), 355.

16. Chambers, *Witness*, 505; Teachout, ed., *Ghosts*, 192.

17. Chambers to Ralph de Toledano, 16 May 1950, de Toledano, ed., *Notes*, 23-25.

18. Tanenhaus, *Chambers*, 474; *National Review*, 5 (18 Jan 1958), 71; Pipe Creek Monthly Meeting, Membership Register, 1881-1997, 3-4, Friends Historical Library, Swarthmore College, Swarthmore College, Swarthmore, Penn., lists the dates of the deaths of both Whittaker and Esther, as though they were still members.

19. Nixon, *Crises*, 425-26; Ingle, *Nixon's First Cover-up*; Logan P. Smith, *Unforgotten Years* (Boston: Little, Brown and Co., 1939), 19, 31. On the Philadelphia Quaker establishment, see E. Digby Baltzell, *Puritan Boston and Quaker Philadelphia: Two Protestant Ethics and the Spirit of Authority and Leadership* (Boston: Beacon Press, 1979).

20. Larry Miller, "Clarence Pickett and the Alger Hiss Case," *Friends Journal*, 40 (Dec 1994), 15; *Friends Journal*, 41 (Feb, Mar 1995), 4, 6

21. But see Hugh Barbour and J. William Frost, *The Quakers* (New York: Greenwood Press, 1988), ch. 20 for some suggestive comments. See also, Chuck Fager, *Remaking Friends: How Progressives Friends Changed Quakerism & Helped Save America* (Durham, N.C.: Kimo Press, 2014) Fager follows the history of an off-shoot of the Hicksites and ventures that their support of the Union cause in the Civil War and flirtations with socialism may have presaged a leftward drift. See also E. Digby Baltzell, *Puritan Boston and Quaker Philadelphia: Two Protestant Ethics and the Spirit of Class Authority and Leadership* (Boston: Beacon Press, 1979). The subject cries out for more research.

22. Chambers, *Witness*, 547.

23. Chambers to William F. Buckley, Jr., 7 Feb, 6 Apr 1954, William F. Buckley, Jr., *Odyssey of a Friend: Whittaker Chambers' Letters to William F. Buckley, Jr., 1954-1961* (New York: G.P. Putnam's Sons, 1969), 49-53, 59-63.

24. Chambers to Willi Schlamm and Buckley, [7 Sep 1954], Buckley, ed., *Odyssey*, 78-84.

25. Teachout, ed., *Ghosts*, 340-44.

26. Chambers to Buckley, Sept 1954, Whittaker Chambers, *Cold Friday* (New York: Random House, 1964), 236-38.

27. Teachout, ed., *Ghosts*, xxvii, 313-18; *National Review*, 5 (1 Feb 1958), 119.

28. Alger Hiss to Elmore Jackson, 13 Aug 1948, General Adm: Individuals: Chambers, Whittaker/Hiss, Alger, 13 Aug 1948, AFSC Archives, Philadelphia, Penn.

Back From The Brink:
North Carolina Yearly Meeting Says No To A Split

Chuck Fager

I

North Carolina Yearly Meeting-FUM (NCYM) has ended the two-year effort to purge its "liberal meetings."

This seems to be the most definite outcome of its showdown annual session on August 13 and 14, 2016.

It was a very close thing. The leadership wanted a purge disguised as a split, and the steamroller machinery was in place. They trundled it up to the brink, and teetered on the edge.

Then they drew back.

That was one of the two most telling items of the session.

That, and the number 8.

We'll get to the number presently; first the walk to the brink. Stay with us.

II

[For those who haven't been following this story, reported on in detail in our issues #26-#28: the purge effort, after simmering for some years, came into the open at the 2014 annual session, with demands from several hard-core evangelical pastors that "liberal" members and meetings in NCYM should "immediately resign." Among the issues that lit the fuse of this outburst were recent public controversies over homosexuality and same sex marriage, as well as other political and theological stances associated with opposing views on these matters. When the targeted Friends stoutly refused to leave (except for one small meeting), the insurgents continued to demand that a way be found to purge them.

Since then, several committees have been formed to deal with this conflict; but none was able to reach anything like unity, especially on proposals to force out those derided as "liberals." In the face of this resistance, more than a dozen evangelically-oriented meetings quit NCYM. Besides the resulting sharp drop in membership, the YM's budget was cut in half by the loss of meeting dues. NCYM's Executive Committee told the body in the fall of 2015 that the conflict threatened the YM's existence, and pointed at the liberals as being the culprits. Yet by the end of 2015, there was still no resolution in sight.]

III

Our last report (in Issue #28) concluded with NCYM's spring Representative session on March 4, 2016. There the "Task Group" (née "Task Force," the latest in a series of *ad hoc* groups) made its second report on "The Way Forward" in the 18-month long effort to purge several "liberal meetings" from the YM. That report did not fare well; liberals did not like some proposals, evangelicals rebuffed others.

The next Representative session was set for June, and maneuvering for it became intense, though mostly conducted more or less clandestinely. In April Yadkin Quarter produced a letter insisting that unless four of the "liberal" meetings were "brought to unity" with Yadkin's understanding of some doctrinal passages in the NCYM Faith & Practice by November, 2016, many of its members were ready to quit NCYM. For weeks this letter's existence was falsely denied by NCYM officials, but rumors about it still spread. Another, shorter letter from Southern Quarter called for the YM to split. (Attachment A includes these letters.)

At about the same time, a group of nine pastors came together, on their own initiative, and decided to negotiate a settlement of the dispute. The group considered itself representative of the main trends in the YM: three "liberal," three "centrist," and three "evangelical." They met privately, but with YM officials in attendance, and talked about what to do.

It was soon evident that the real goal of at least some was to engineer a split in the YM, figuring the large majority of meetings would gather into a strongly evangelical group, with a small rump of liberals on the other; it was essentially a purge in disguise. As this agenda became clear, one of the nine pastors left the group, and another dissented strongly. Nonetheless, the other seven drafted a letter proposing such a split and submitted it to the Executive Committee. As they wrote: "The statement was made in our discussions that 'we are going to separate in love or we are going to separate in anger.' We choose love." (Their proposal is Attachment B.)

This was just what the Executive Committee (EC) leadership wanted to hear, and they wrote up their own their own proposal for a split (which is Attachment C). The EC plan closely resembled the model of the Indiana purge (recounted in QT's Issues #18 - #24.) The EC adopted this plan for a split despite the fact that two of its members dissented, and a third not only objected but resigned in protest. Such is what passed for "unity" there.

The EC brought its proposal to the June Representative session, and presented it as only a matter for discussion, rather than action. They added to the pressure for it by reporting that two more meetings had left NCYM, making for a total of 17 since the struggle had surfaced in 2014. The body agreed to have the EC prepare a plan for how to discuss all that would be involved in a separation for consideration at the Annual Session, set for August 13-14.

At least, that is what some attenders were permitted to believe. Others, mainly those determined to press for a purge by whatever name, came away convinced that they could get agreement to launch the separation in August, make it a done deal, with only bureaucratic details to be worked out.

But the EC's actual plan, dated July 20 (which is Attachment D), was something very different from the discussion document promised in June: it was in fact committed to the launching of a split at Annual Session.

As the July plan circulated, doubts arose, including some about the EC's trustworthiness. To some it looked as though the plan was now being put on a fast track in a bait-and-switch move, likely in order to be able to have a split definitely underway by November, to meet the Yadkin deadline, and to make a pitch for some of the departed meetings to return to the "purified" evangelical successor.

But pushback wasn't long in coming. Several meetings issued minutes announcing firm opposition to a split (two such statements are in Attachment E). And there were murmurs from others.

When the Annual Session's main business session convened, among the items the Clerk noted was that two more meetings had left NCYM, making the total now 19. This added to the leadership's sense of urgency to take some kind of decisive action. Some who didn't like the idea feared that the fix was in, that the leadership would declare the split approved, Indiana-style, using the "voice vote" maneuver by which they altered Faith & Practice irregularly in November of 2015, ignoring dissent, as reported in QT #28.

But before they moved for approval, the Clerk called for the group to break down into smaller circles, with EC members as facilitators, to ensure all members had a chance to speak, and copious notes were to be taken.

When all this was done, and the notes were reviewed by the EC, they came to the reassembled group with a confession: they needed to consult some more, and even redraft their proposal in light of what Friends had expressed. This would, they thought, take fifteen minutes or so.

The group huddled in a corner, and leaned heavily on the skills of Tom Terrell, an EC member and an attorney, for a redraft. They were hard at it for more than an hour.

And when they returned again, and their new version was read, it was different. They noted that they had proposed a split.

"However," the EC acknowledged, "we did not hear a sufficiently strong consensus for unity" behind the split. (And in plain Quaker speech, and honest Quaker process, an "insufficiently strong consensus for unity" is really no "consensus for unity" at all.) But the EC still felt that something must be done. So instead they urged the YM to "reorganize" itself to accommodate the persisting differences.

Reorganize how? In truth, they didn't know. But they thought there was promise in adapting a model that had been floated twice in 2015, of forming two "associations" within NCYM, and maintaining the central structure as a kind of umbrella holding company. It would supervise NCYM endowments, property, and Quaker Lake Camp.

And how long would this "reorganization" take? That too was uncertain.

The very vagueness of this proposal was appealing to some key Friends in the body – it bespoke a humility that made for a refreshing contrast to the succession of demands and ultimatums that had battered them for so long. Representatives of two of the targeted "liberal" meetings rose to say they thought they could live with a "reorganization." (The text of the EC minute is in Attachment F)

What does this plan offer? For those (who are more numerous than either the "Gang of Seven" pastors or the EC realized) who are uncomfortable with the theological/cultural diversity of the remaining Friends in NCYM – and yet unwilling to go through a split, they can turn to a new association to find a congenial group to relate to (a "safe space", to borrow a liberal phrase). That's something they don't feel they have in the status quo. And the liberals get an end to the purge effort.

Further, those who find their meetings are already "diverse" need not be forced to squeeze them into a new straitjacket. The turn away from an enforced choice of "sheep" vs "goats" was underlined when a pastor asked, what if his meeting didn't want to identify with either of the two proposed new sub-associations? Would it be able to "float free" within the YM, as before?

The EC assured him it could, that ultimate decisions about the "reorganization" and its shape would stay with local meetings: "Within this plan of reorganization," the minute declared, "each meeting's destiny will be controlled and determined by the meeting itself, and each resulting organization will determine its own theological identity."

The Clerk announced approval. While uncertainty about specifics remained, a sense of relief was palpable.

At the closing session on Sunday August 14, the YM message acknowledged the depth and cost of the differences that had brought NCYM to this point. But it concluded that

> "Out of the chaos and lack of clarity, in an effort to work with Love without compromising Faith, Friends approved a

way to move forward. NCYM-FUM will work on reorganizing with subgroups or associations remaining under one yearly meeting umbrella. We intend to remain joined in essential ministries that are important to all, staying in relationship with each other, while we seek clarity of our theological distinctives for the groups that comprise the yearly meeting." (Full text in attachment G)

IV

Despite the uncertainty about how NCYM will now evolve, the end of the two-year crusade to purge "liberals" is definite. (That's not to say future purge efforts could not happen. These outbreaks seem to have a cyclical character; they're a kind of organizational bipolar disorder. But for now, the purge has been set aside; and in our judgment, that's a big deal.)

As this reality sinks in, there may be some more departures. At least one meeting, Cedar Square, sent their representative to the annual session to read a letter filled with a tired rehash of bible quotes about the infiltration of false apostles and prophets, workers for satan and the anti-christ, etc., who all had to be condemned and steered clear of. Little attention was paid to this missive, even though presumably it is a prelude to departure.

And others? Asked about the likely reaction from meetings in Yadkin Quarter, which issued the November deadline, the group's Clerk said that some would likely accept the new stance, and some might not. (Which fulfills the timeless insight of the prophet Yogi Berra, that "predictions are hard, especially about the future.")

V

Why did the EC back away from the split?

The process remains somewhat mysterious; here are some speculations:

First of all, at the annual session the EC was confronted, not by a conveniently packaged group of four scapegoat "liberal" meetings to dispose of, but objections from, by an informal count, at least ten. Not that a large group has suddenly "gone liberal"; but more than one Representative agreed with the concerns raised by the dean of NCYM pastors, Wade Craven of Randleman Meeting.

Craven's meeting is in the heart of Southern Quarter, where split sentiment has been strong; yet he has been there for fifty years, and along the way, he said, his thinking on many matters has evolved. Perhaps most important, he saw clearly that his own meeting was "diverse" about many matters, and deciding whether to join a split would likely stir up discord in the congregation – and why should they subject themselves to that? (The same sentiment was behind the other pastor's question about whether his meeting would be obliged to join one of the new "associations"; that decision would also be difficult and divisive; so why make it?)

In sum, a decision to split NCYM would export conflict into many meetings which did not have or want it, regardless of what they thought about liberal notions in other places. There was indeed no "consensus" to accept such an export.

The wonder here is that it took the EC so long to get this message. After all, for two years, one ad hoc committee and task force has followed another in an effort to square the circle of the demand for a purge met by the targets' doughty refusal to buckle. The urge to follow the Indiana plan, of twisting Quaker process to silence opposition and force it through, was clearly strong; but in the end, it did not prevail. Perhaps the key EC members remembered just in time that the Indiana purge was initially aimed at a single meeting, and it ended by driving away seventeen.

Even in the weeks between the March and the June Representative sessions, the EC had had ample opportunity to discern the lack of "consensus for unity." After all their "Gang of Nine/Seven" pastors proved a bust, indeed a fiasco, coming up with a proposal that did not fly, and which was rejected by two of their own number. That outcome was not at all a "consensus for unity"; but they didn't want to see it. Then in the EC itself, two members strongly dissented from the split idea, and another resigned in protest. Same deal.

Finally, when the chorus got loud enough at the annual session, it seemed to sink in. Does that attest to the power of repetition? Sheer exhaustion? Or perhaps grace?

Whichever, they have now given themselves a chance at–if not a new start, at least a new chapter. The "reorganization" conversations will begin with one major advantage: the purge threat will be absent. Without that sword hanging over them, who knows how differently the protagonists/antagonists might be able to hear each other? Might they discover things on which they agree (in practice they have); or even to peaceably agree to disagree?

There are no guarantees. The urge for splitting and self-destruction could surface again. Yet if they do manage to change the climate of interaction, then perhaps NCYM Friends can begin to address the second major item mentioned at the beginning, the important and portentous number 8.

That figure emerged on the last day, in the report on the Young Friends program at the annual session. The "youth pastor" speaking for them noted that there were many fun activities and amenities available at the summer camp where they were gathered, and the YFs enjoyed them – all eight of them on hand.

Hearing that number jerked this writer to full attention. *Eight?* Ten minus two? Eight was the total number of teenagers who could be enticed or inveigled to show up?

It was not so long ago that this YF turnout was well in three figures. And for that matter, the number 175, in the NCYM Epistle, added punch to the arithmetic. That's how many attended the 2016 annual session overall. In 2013, only three years ago, the minutes record that attendance was in excess of 400, more than twice as many. The number of YFs was not broken out, but I well remember seeing large numbers of them.

These numbers were not official until after the session approved the "reorganization" minute. One wonders if the EC saw them coming; or rather, not coming.

Yet this collapse should have been no surprise. After all, the main topic of conversation in and around NCYM for two years has been: how can we make people go away? It's hard to imagine an atmosphere more likely to turn off and alienate people of all ages, particularly anyone who feels spiritually vulnerable and is seeking freedom to explore and establish their own religious identities.

A conversation about this among the diverse Friends who choose to remain in NCYM as this "reorganization" takes shape, has a chance to be very different. Only a chance; but that is more than they have had in a long time.

VI

As the "reorganization" conversations get underway this autumn, there are a number of items that will loom large. None is insoluble; but none can be safely ignored. Here's our first-cut list:

1. Devolve the recording of pastors. For years the NCYM Recording committee has been a locus and flashpoint of factional maneuver and struggle. Its work has sown long-festering grievances and resentments, and has hardly assured a high quality of hires. So enough is enough. Delegating that task to local meetings, as the Baptists do, would likely be the safest option; or leaving it to the associations.

2. Loosen the grip on Quaker Lake Camp. Reports from staff and board make clear that to survive, QLC has to become more autonomous and greatly broaden its marketing effort. When NCYM's YF turnout drops below ten at annual session, the body can hardly hope to fill the camp. While QLC can still maintain some loose ties with NCYM, autonomy is its future, if it's to have one.

3. Watch the money, and use most of it for pensions. Just as NCYM's shrinkage means there are fewer youth to send to camp, it has also left many fewer donors to support the fund for retired pastors. But seeing this obligation is met is something that most Friends can agree on. Thus much of NCYM's income needs to go there, to fill its huge funding gap. Yes, pension checks are not as

exciting as glitzy new mission projects; but it only seems that way, until you need the checks.

4. Also about money: keep the NCYM "holding company" a bare bones operation; if there's extra funds after overhead and pensions, divide it proportionally, and let meetings and their associations organize and support their own cooperative projects. That will also avoid many needless conflicts.

5. When a new General Secretary is hired, make sure (and make public) that she/he is committed to the reorganized YM project, and not some poser with pockets full of hidden factional agendas.

6. Keep the reorganization process open! Resist the chronic temptation to get a few selected "insiders" (especially pastors) together to hash things out privately. Make sure instead that rank and file members see and hear what the Executive Committee is doing, while they're doing it, not just every three or six months in settled, take-it-or-leave-it packages. Let's not waste the lessons of the "Gang of Nine/Seven" fiasco, the expulsion explosion of September 2015 or the other failed committees, which are 1) there is no such spiritual elite group in NCYM; and 2) there are no shortcuts around the laborious work of building real "sufficient unity" for a genuine Quaker "consensus."

7. That business of the "instant revision" of Faith & Practice in November last year to make the YM supreme over local meetings – maybe it can now be quietly left on hold? After all, the EC has just gone on record, with group approval, guaranteeing meetings autonomy about what to do with the reorganization. If the committee means it, that's a practical rollback of that provision; which is a good idea.

8. Don't panic about the disappearance of young people. But don't give up, either. Face it: it will take time to get over two years of a YM agenda devoted in fact to driving people away. If NCYM recovers and gets past that, there's some more bad news to swallow: most even relatively "happy" churches are losing young people too. The number of alarmed analyses of this exodus can crowd your bookshelf and stuff your email inbox; consultants are lined up to fill your weekends with high-priced seminars and workshops about it, and snake oil quick fixes are priced like EpiPens – except at least the EpiPen actually works. Yet there are some church groups that are growing and holding on to youth. Are you ready for the list? Mormons, Amish, very Orthodox Jews, and some Muslim groups. Growing. Could NCYM learn something and maybe adapt some "best practices" from them. I doubt it will be easy.

9. Finally, don't lose your nerve. No doubt at least a few more meetings will likely depart rather than accept the body's decision. Swallow hard, and let them go. Then if some claque of hardliners comes with another ultimatum, quietly hand it back to them and move on; NCYM has other, better work to do.

As the EC's minute says, there will likely be more ideas and concerns come up. And there are no guarantees of success. But at least this time, we can end a report on a cautiously hopeful note.

Attachments

Attachment A: Yadkin & Southern Quarter letters.

Attachment B: Three Letters detailing the proposal by the "Gang of Nine - or Seven" pastors.

Attachment C: Executive Committee Split Proposal #1, June 4, 2016

Attachment D: Executive Committee Split Proposal #2, July 2016

Attachment E: Two Dissents from the EC Plan for Separation

Attachment F: Minute of Reorganization, August 13, 2016

Attachment G: NCYM 2016 Epistle

(Attachment A: Yadkin & Southern Quarter letters.)

Yadkin Valley Quarterly Meeting of the Religious Society of Friends
in session at Harmony Grove Friends Meeting
Fourth month, seventeenth day, 2016

[TO] Hugh Spaulding, Clerk of NCYM Ministry and Counsel
Mike Fulp, Sr., Clerk of NCYM Representative Body

Friends,

Yadkin Valley Quarterly Meeting of the Religious Society of Friends, Ministry and Counsel, in session fourth month, seventeenth day, 2016 gave much discussion to the current disunity of Friends in North Carolina Yearly Meeting. Many Monthly Meetings have already left the Yearly Meeting and many more are ready to leave if unity in our theological beliefs is not accomplished soon. We have reaffirmed our Faith and Practice more than once that speaks to "a personal faith in Jesus Christ as our Savior" yet we have not resolved the division that is present.

Yadkin Valley Quarterly Meeting Ministry and Counsel approved the following minute:

> "We expect that Meetings come to unity with Jesus Christ of the Scriptures and the Faith statements in Faith and Practice (Faith and Thought chapter, 2012 edition p.27). If not we recommend that those Meetings be sanctioned and or disciplined, with possible disownment, by the November 2016 Representative Body session. Meetings of concern include: New Garden, Spring, First Friends of Greensboro, and Winston-Salem Friends."

Our Ministry and Counsel brought this recommendation to the general Quarterly Meeting session held immediately following the Ministry and Counsel session and the recommendation was approved by this body to be sent to both North Carolina Yearly Meeting Ministry and Counsel and North Carolina Yearly Meeting Representative Body.

If you have questions or need any clarification you may contact me or Stanley Todd, Presiding Clerk of the Ministry and Counsel. His email is lftxdx7@yahoo.com and mine is jcxritxt36@yaktel.org . My phone is 702-536-5995. Thank you for your consideration of this.

In His Service,

Judy C Ritter, Presiding Clerk Yadkin Valley Quarterly Meeting

cc. Don Farlow, Superintendent

Harmony Grove Friends Monthly Meeting
Branon Friends Monthly Meeting
Hunting Creek Friends Monthly Meeting
The Connection @ Ballantyne
Mount Carmel Friends Monthly Meeting
Deep Creek Friends Monthly Meeting
Statesville Friends Monthly Meeting
Forbush Friends Monthly Meeting
Winthrop Friends Monthly Meeting

Southern Quarterly Meeting

Asheboro Back Creek Bethel Randleman Science Hill Cedar Square Hopewell Marlboro South Plainfield Thomasville

5th Month, 21st Day, 2016,

To our Friends on the NCYM Executive Committee,

In a Spirit of Love and Concern, because North Carolina Yearly Meeting has continuing significant Theological differences, Southern Quarterly Meeting asks that the Executive Committee put forward a plan of separation beginning at the 6th Month, 4th Day, 2016 Representative Body Meeting.

Roger Greene, Presiding Clerk, Southern Quarter

(Attachment B: Three Letters detailing the proposal by the "Gang of Nine - or Seven" pastors.)

Undated letter (likely early April)

Dear Friends of North Carolina Yearly Meeting,

Recently a few pastors felt a leading to come together and have a conversation about the direction and future of our beloved Yearly Meeting. We recognize that Friends are exhausted and much energy has been expended. We also know that there has been much pain throughout this whole journey. For that reason, we felt it was important to come together and seek discernment as to a way forward.

To that end, a group of pastors have agreed to come together on Thursday, April 14th, at Quaker Lake and have a conversation that hopefully will lead to clarity and way forward. These pastors include: Scott Wagoner, Margaret Webb, Deborah Suess, Terry Venable, David Hobson, Mike Wall, Eric Morrison, and Mike Butler. We have sought to represent the diversity of our Yearly Meeting and our hope is to have a loving and productive conversation about our future. We do not intend to try and convince one another of who is right and who is wrong. That has felt to be a dead end road and we want to move beyond that point. We have intentionally kept this initial group small in order to facilitate the dialogue. We certainly hope it will lead to further conversations that involve more folks.

We have shared our intentions with our Interim Superintendent, Don Farlow. Along with Don Farlow, we have also invited Brent McKinney, Hugh Spaulding, Judy Ritter, and Michael Fulp, Sr. to be in attendance as a listening and prayerful presence. We hope that Friends will view this as a sincere attempt to move our Yearly Meeting forward in a positive manner and not as an attempt to undermine any work that has been accomplished up to now.

Most of all, we ask for your prayers as this group gathers. We ask that you pray for wisdom, insight, and clarity as well as the willingness to be present to one another and listen deeply. If you have any questions, please feel free to contact Scott Wagoner, Deborah Suess, Margaret Webb, or Terry Venable.

In Christ's Peace,

(Listing of Pastors)

Letter after their first session.(Addressed to "pastors"; unclear to whom it was actually sent; does not seem to have circulated widely.)

To: NCYM Pastors
Re: April 14 Gathering at Quaker Lake / Follow-up Letter

Seeking a Way Forward in NCYM

As mentioned in a recent letter to NC Yearly Meeting Pastors, a small group of pastors representing the diversity of NCYM came together for a frank conversation about the direction and future of our Yearly Meeting in light of the Yearly Meeting body's inability to move toward an agreeable resolution to our recent conflict, and to discern a way forward. The pastors in attendance were Mike Butler, David Hobson, Frank Massey, Eric Morrison, Deborah Suess, Terry Venable, Scott Wagoner, Mike Wall, and Margaret Webb. In addition to the pastors, Don Farlow, Interim Superintendent; Mike Fulp, Sr., Presiding Clerk; Brent McKinney, Clerk of Executive Committee; Hugh Spaulding, Clerk of Ministry & Counsel; and Judy Ritter, Clerk of the Task Group, were also in attendance to observe and provide a prayerful presence.

The group discussed several things that unite us and bring us together as Christians and Quakers. Among the things acknowledged included relationships that have been cultivated over many years, works of service and mission such as Friends Disaster Service, MOWA Choctaw, and other service/mission opportunities, Quaker Lake Camp and the decades of life changing ministry that has taken place, and our shared endowments which have been built from the faithful stewardship of so many members of North Carolina Yearly Meeting.

While we can celebrate much that unites us, we were also able to name the issues that divide us. These places of division include the authority of Scripture, how one understands the atonement of Christ and salvation, same gender marriage, and the inability to form a united corporate identity. We recognize that the gulf is wide, and that for most of the individuals and congregations in our Yearly Meeting, these points of conflict and division are impenetrable as well as non-negotiable.

After a time of silence, prayer, and discussion, the group began to ask some challenging questions: Can we all stay together in loving Christian fellowship? Do we have enough common ground and unity of purpose to continue to be part of the same Yearly Meeting? If so, how? If not, how can we proceed and move forward in a way that all meetings feel honored and valued? The conversation was difficult at times, but always in a spirit of love and good will toward one another, and always with the ultimate goal of discerning the Spirit of Christ for all of North Carolina Yearly Meeting.

After a lengthy period of conversation and dialogue, we came to the realization that the differences are great and that the only way forward that seemed to bring any degree of resolution would require a mutually agreed upon separation//reorganization that seeks to value and respect the other. This reorganization would allow for greater unity of purpose and mission and would allow all of our congregations to move forward in doing the work of Christ as they feel led. While most of the pastors discerned this as the most plausible way forward, pastoral minister, David Hobson, still did not feel that separation was the only way and that we need to keep trying to find ways to stay together.

We also believe, hope, and pray that there are ways in which we can work together, and remain connected on some levels. We are hopeful that we can stay connected through those things that do unite us, and set at liberty for each group those things that divide us. It may be possible to stay together in relation to those things that bring us all vitality, energy, and life, like, Quaker Lake, Friends Disaster Service, Quaker Men, USFW, to mention a few.

It needs to be noted that this group has no authority. It has not been nominated or asked by North Carolina Yearly Meeting to accomplish any specific task. We gathered only as individual pastors that love our Yearly Meeting, and are concerned about our current situation. These same folks do plan a follow-up meeting to discern what next steps, if any, can be suggested to the Yearly Meeting. We share these letters only as a way of providing full disclosure and transparency. We also know that for our conversations to become a reality, much work will need to be accomplished that will take time and effort. But even more, it will require prayer. Please pray with us that God will show us the right path and the way forward.

In Christ's Peace,

Scott Wagoner
Terry Venable

Proposal to NCYM Executive Committee
Monday, May 9th, 2016

On April 14th, 2016 and again on May 4th, 2016, a small group of concerned pastors, that represent the diversity of NCYM, chose to come together for a frank conversation about the direction and future of our Yearly Meeting, seeking to discern a way forward that could bring to a conclusion the recent conflict that has dominated North Carolina Yearly Meeting. In those meetings, we recognized and celebrated those things which unite us and bring us life. Among the things highlighted include relationships that have been cultivated over many years, works of service and mission such as Friends Disaster Service, Mowa Choctaw, and other service/mission opportunities, Quaker Lake Camp and the decades of life changing ministry that has taken place there, and our shared endowments which have been built from the faithful stewardship of so many members of North Carolina Yearly Meeting.

In the context of those discussions, we also recognized that there are theological differences which divide us. And those theological understandings are fundamental to each person and meeting living out their faith with integrity. As part of our conversation and process of discernment, it became clear to most of the group that some form of separation or restructuring of NCYM is not only necessary but inevitable.(It should be noted that two of the original nine pastors were not in unity with this conclusion, and are hopeful and prayerful that NCYM could remain together fully.)[Parenthesis in original.]

Therefore we as a group of concerned pastors/Friends make the following proposal to the NCYM Executive Committee for your consideration:

1. That NCYM divide into two groups around the different understandings of the role of Faith & Practice and Scripture. The goal should be for the long term sustainability of both groups, and the hope that each group would be free to live out their faith and more fully engage in ministry that is life giving to each group.

2. That a transition team be named to oversee this process, make sure all groups and meetings are appropriately represented and respected, examine any legal issues, and bring recommendations about specifics

of the plan to NCYM Representative Body and Yearly Meeting Sessions. The transition team should include Yearly Meeting leadership, and other representative members. Our group would like to be involved in the process of transition, and the following individuals have expressed a willingness to serve in such a capacity: Mike Butler, Deborah Suess, Terry Venable, Scott Wagoner, and Mike Wall.

3. On a temporary basis, both groups would remain as members of NCYM, as a legal and fiduciary entity. As such, current levels of support would remain for Quaker Lake and the Pastor's Retirement Fund, with provisions to establish a timeline and plan for Quaker Lake's autonomy and long-term sustainability, and to determine a plan for the pension fund and other NCYM endowments. And we are prayerful that we can continue to work together, and continue to find life and vitality in those that have always united us, as we have worked and ministered as the body of Christ.

Our group does not make this recommendation lightly. We all love and support North Carolina Yearly Meeting, and we all also love and support the meetings we serve. The statement was made in our discussions that "we are going to separate in love or we are going to separate in anger." We choose love.

Thank you for your willingness to consider this proposal. We believe and pray that it is Spirit-led, and comes only after a process of discernment. We offer it to you for further discernment. Much work is still to be done. And much work is still to be done by the meetings of NCYM. Blessings to you all in the task and work that you have undertaken for our Yearly Meeting.

In the Love of Jesus Christ,
Mike Butler, Eric Morrison, Deborah Suess, Terry Venable, Scott Wagoner, Mike Wall, and Margaret Webb

(Attachment C: Executive Committee Split Proposal #1, June 4, 2016)

Executive Committee Recommendation to the
Representative Body of the North Carolina Yearly Meeting
June 4, 2016 [Approved]

The Executive Committee of the North Carolina Yearly Meeting of the Religious Society of Friends met in special sessions on the 9th and 31st days of the Fifth Month, 2016, in the spirit of love and prayerful discernment and in focused attention on matters of both faith and practice that have caused labored discussions among North Carolina Friends for many years.

The Executive Committee acknowledges the differences among Friends in the North Carolina Yearly Meeting that are continuous and unabating regarding the use of Scripture and the freedom available to interpret Scripture through leadings of the Holy Spirit; the autonomy of individuals and individual meetings within the broader authority of the Yearly Meeting, and whether the Yearly Meeting has or should have authority to discipline meetings for what are determined to be departures from Faith and Practice.

And while being dutifully mindful of our origins in the traveling ministries of George Fox and William Edmundson, who visited this colony in 1672, and of the proud history and accomplishments of early Friends who settled here in the 1600s and who later formed the North Carolina Yearly Meeting to bind together the growing communities of Friends across this state and beyond, the Committee listened again to the many voices of concern or discontent expressed in the missives and letters from individuals, Meetings, and Quarterly Meetings that have accumulated in recent months, and recounted the meetings that have elected to depart from the Yearly Meeting within the past year.

Determining that our differences are insurmountable and will impede the future growth and detract from the ministries of the Yearly Meeting, the Executive Committee recommends to the Representative Body assembled that the member meetings of North Carolina Yearly Meeting patiently commit to an orderly, deliberate, compassionate, and mutually respectful plan of separation into two yearly meetings, and in that plan of separation, allow each meeting, if it chooses, to join either of the two new yearly meetings, however organized, which can be life- giving for all of our monthly meetings.
We further recognize that, if the Committee's recommendation is approved by the Representative Body, a carefully structured

discussion must occur that would consider matters of (1) faith (2) organization (3) property, and (4) law, and that this discussion must include multiple voices and viewpoints within the Yearly Meeting.

Given the complexity of questions to be asked and matters to consider, the Executive Committee further recommends that the Executive Committee shall be delegated the limited task of identifying and organizing the components of the deliberate discussion that would necessarily follow, and to return to Annual Session with recommendations for consideration by the Yearly Meeting that pertain to process only, with substantive discussions to occur in carefully selected committees to follow Annual Session.

We do not propose a timeline or a deadline. We only propose that the process should commence, and that it should occur with due care and in the spirit of Christ's love and mutual respect one to another. Our recommendation is not complete without the notation that three members of the Executive Committee expressed their decision to "stand aside" if the rest of the Committee proceeded with this recommendation.

Respectfully submitted this 4th day of the Sixth Month, 2016.

D. Brent McKinney, Clerk

(Attachment D: Executive Committee Split Proposal #2, July 2016)

July 20, 2016
From: Executive Committee

To: Ministry and Counsel Clerks, Monthly Meeting Clerks, and Pastors

As requested at the Representative Body meeting on June 4th, the Executive Committee has created a Procedural Plan that will explore the possibilities of separating the North Carolina Yearly Meeting into two yearly meetings. Upon approval of the Plan at the upcoming Annual Sessions and successful completion of the procedures set forth in the Plan, the current NCYM will become two
independent yearly meetings at the conclusion of the 2017 Annual Sessions.
Please review the enclosed/attached Draft Procedural Plan and bring all questions, comments and concerns to the Annual Business Session on Saturday morning, August 13.

D. Brent McKinney, Clerk

DRAFT

North Carolina Yearly Meeting of Friends
Procedural Plan for Separation into Two Yearly Meetings
July 14, 2016

Time Period*   Action

June 4, 2016 – North Carolina Yearly Meeting gave approval at the meeting of representatives on June 4, 2016 to move forward with the development of a procedural plan to separate into two yearly meetings.

June 23– Executive Committee asked the NCYM Ministry and Counsel to develop statements of faith for two yearly meetings. One statement would focus on "authority" and the other statement would focus on "autonomy." The EC also asked M & C to present the draft statements to representatives at the annual M & C meeting for discussion on August 6th.

The two statements of faith, including subsequent revisions, will be included in the Procedural Plan report at annual sessions for presentation on Saturday, August 13th.

July 14 – The Executive Committee reviewed and revised a "draft procedural plan" to separate into two yearly meetings and approved of sending the draft report to all monthly meetings.

August 13 – The Procedural Plan, including the two draft statements of faith, will be presented at annual sessions for consideration of approval by the gathered body of representatives.

Until NCYM is separated into two yearly meetings, all members currently serving on committees, boards, as NCYM representatives, and other volunteer capacities should continue to serve in their current position. The NCYM Nominating Committee should only fill vacancies where needed and upon request from the committee or board.

August 14 – Nov. 5 – If the plan is approved, each Monthly Meeting will be asked to align with their preference for one of the two yearly meetings. The statements of faith will be central to the alignments. Each monthly meeting will notify the NCYM Ministry and Counsel and the Superintendent of its decision.

Also, each quarter will appoint a representative to serve on a committee that will discuss quarter alignments.

The committee should consider the number of meetings in each quarter, the number of members in each quarter, the travel distance to quarterly meetings, and the general compatibility of the meetings. A plan of alignment should be presented to the NCYM Ministry and Counsel. A progress report will be given by M&C at the November meeting of representatives.

The Trustees, Trustees of Trust Funds, Finance Committee, and Superintendent will develop a minimum of three (3) conceptual scenarios showing how all investment funds, endowment(s), properties and other assets will be utilized by the two yearly meetings in the future. The committee will be chaired by the chairperson of the Trustees. These conceptual scenarios should be submitted to the NCYM Office prior to the November 5th meeting of representatives. The conceptual scenarios will be presented for discussion and consideration of approval, if ready.

Nov. 5 – March 4 – The new interim quarterly meetings of each yearly meeting will appoint members to serve on two committees, a Faith and Practice Development/Revision Committee and a Nominating Committee. The committees will begin to work soon thereafter for the development/revision of a Faith and Practice for each yearly meeting and for the appointment of members to serve on selected committees, boards, and as representatives of the yearly meeting.

Each monthly meeting within the new interim quarterly meetings and the new yearly meetings are encouraged to discuss and consider the ministries and missions of the current yearly meeting which they would like to undertake. As we prepare to separate, maintenance of the NCYM ministries, missions and programs will be a significant challenge and may need to be handled by the monthly meetings, quarters or new yearly meetings.

This may not be a bad outcome as the quarters are commonly viewed by many members as our weakest link. Current ministries and missions include but are not limited to; Jamaica, Mexico, MOWA, FUM (Samburu, Friends Theological College, Turkana, Belize, Ramallah), YWAM, YFAC, missionaries, evangelism, Christian Education, Missions (enhanced at the local level), Publications, Care of Records, Christian Vocations, Creative Aging, Cemeteries, Quaker Lake and additional youth activities. A summary report of the discussions should be submitted to the Executive Committee. (The outcome of these discussions will have an impact on the respective "askings" of each new yearly meeting.")

Monthly Meetings will continue the discernment process of alignment with a yearly meeting.

The Trustees, Trustees of Trust Funds, Finance Committee and Superintendent will continue development of the scenarios as related to the assets of the yearly meeting and prepare a detailed plan of "actions to be taken" for implementation of each conceptual scenario, or for the preferred scenario,
if known.

March 4 – June 3 – The Trustees, Trustees of Trust Funds, Finance Committee and Superintendent will submit a final plan to the Executive Committee for the preferred scenario and utilization of all assets, going forward.

All monthly meetings should discern final alignment with one of the two yearly meetings and submit their decision to M & C.

The Executive Committee should receive reports from each new interim quarter regarding their proposed undertaking of ministries and missions.

Faith and Practice Development/Revision Committees should submit their proposed Faith and Practice to M&C.

With the information received from "multiple voices," the Executive Committee will prepare a Draft Declaration of Separation including, monthly meeting alignments, new quarter alignments, the proposed activities of each quarter, the basic contents of each Faith and Practice, and the proposed utilization of all assets.

June 3–Annual Sessions – The proposed DRAFT "Declaration of Separation" will be presented to all quarters, Committees, Boards, USFW, QM, Ministers Association, and other appropriate groups for review, discussion and comments.

2017 Annual Sessions (Tentative: August 11 – 13) – A Final Declaration of Separation will be presented by the Executive Committee for consideration of approval by the gathered body of representatives.

Upon approval of the Declaration of Separation, each yearly meeting will begin operation in accordance with its Faith and Practice.

* The Executive Committee will provide oversight and guidance for development of the Declaration of Separation and may need to flex the schedule as we move along to accommodate for unforeseen matters or indecision.

(Attachment E: Two Dissents from the EC Plan for Separation)

Jamestown Friends Meeting

June 28, 2016

Clerk of NCYM – FUM
Executive Committee
Superintendent of NCYM
4811 Hilltop Rd
Greensboro NC 27407

Jamestown Friends Meeting, at its regularly scheduled meeting for worship with attention to business, had a lengthy discussion concerning the Executive Committee and Representative Body and the proposal to split or divide the Yearly Meeting. Jamestown Friends Meeting does not and never has supported the concept of dividing or splitting the Yearly Meeting. There are many reasons for this position, but suffice it to say it will only render two groups (or more) worse off than now, will divide meetings and families, and will create hostility and dissention.

It appears that the Quaker process has been abandoned or failed at many levels of the Yearly Meeting. The process of sense of the meeting does not involve voting or head counting. It respects the role of the minority and recognizes that working together is difficult but that is what God call us to do. It requires respect for one another, openness to listen, time to reflect and study, and attempts to find reconciliation, forgiveness and love. It is not based upon pre-set conditions or prepared oratory. It includes quiet listening, searching and openness. It is a slow process at times and is designed to be that way, if necessary.

We, as a meeting, urge our leaders to take as much time as may be needed to hear all views, to treat each other with respect, to make efforts to heal and unify rather than abuse and divide. We seek to find how to help others see our vision of God's work and how we can better understand the vision of others—then hearts and minds may work together to find unity in the Spirit.
On behalf of Jamestown Friends Meeting and with the approval of the monthly meeting,

(signed) Mark Farlow, Frank Massey, Clarence Mattocks

(Editor's note: Mark Farlow is presiding clerk of monthly meeting, Frank Massey is pastor of the meeting, and Clarence Mattocks is clerk of the Peace and Social Concerns Committee.)

From Spring Friends Meeting:

"After careful consideration, Spring Monthly Meeting is agreed that we are unable to support or take part in any plan to divide North Carolina Yearly Meeting.
Such a plan is contrary to the commitments and values we stated in our Ninth Month 2014 letter to Friends, and which we still affirm.
That letter is available online at: http://bit.ly/1QdRsmt. "

A pertinent snippet from Spring's 2014 Letter: "We [at Spring] believe that unity is best achieved by embracing of our diversity and not through the cleavage of our association from others over doctrinal matters."

(Attachment F: Minute of Reorganization, August 13, 2016)

Minute of Reorganization
of the
North Carolina Yearly Meeting of the Religious Society of Friends

August 13, 2016

Over the past 319 years, the North Carolina Yearly Meeting has never been without a time when we debated who we were as Christians and as Quakers; and the steps that we should take to fulfill the missions of Christ on earth.

As the years have become decades and the decades have become centuries, the multiple views and competing positions in this discussion have moved farther apart. The challenge of bridging our differences has become an increasingly daunting task.

In recent years, the chorus of voices concerned about our differences has risen, and we have labored diligently to find a way to maintain our unity of purpose, our unity of worship, and the unity of our corporate body.

Managing this conversation has become a regular task of the Yearly Meeting's Executive Committee, to the exclusion of other work for which we have been appointed. After many meetings, and after long and prayerful discussions, the Executive Committee concludes that matters within our yearly meeting are moving too swiftly for us to assume a posture of organizational inertia.

In just the past year, 19 of our 72 meetings have left the Yearly Meeting and two meetings have been laid down. A diverse group of ministers has asked the Executive Committee to recommend a structured pathway to separation. Southern Quarter has united in asking that we consider taking steps towards division. And we have been informed that several more meetings will leave the Yearly Meeting if action leading to reorganization or division is not quick and decisive.

This afternoon the Executive Committee listened attentively to the questions raised and comments made during morning breakout sessions. We know much more now than we did prior to annual session regarding the beliefs, the fears, the anxieties, and the aspirations of represented meetings.

However, we did not hear a sufficiently strong consensus for unity, and therefore we return to you, as your Executive Committee, seeking approval of the plan as broadly outlined at this morning's session, but with a focus on reorganization rather than separation.

Based on the collective suggestions made in each of your groups, the plan may look differently as we take measured and considered steps towards a reorganized body. At each step, our recommendations and decisions will be made according to your input and approval, and they will be taken in a manner that respects the needs and interests of all members of our Yearly Meeting.

We know that there questions to which we do not yet have answers and that there is now and will later be uncertainty, but as we acknowledge our depleted ranks and consider the rising volume of dissatisfied voices, we conclude that our only reasonable option is to work towards reorganization in whatever form it takes. Within this plan of reorganization, each meeting's destiny will be controlled and determined by the meeting itself, and each resulting organization will determine its own theological identity.

In the face of these many, unknowns and in the Spirit of the same Christ that brought us together 319 years ago, we ask this body to approve the plan presented this morning, but with a focus on reorganization into two groups.

Approved this 13th day, eight month, 2016.

Mike Fulp, Presiding Clerk
NCYM

(Attachment G: NCYM 2016 Epistle)

North Carolina Yearly Meeting Epistle -319th Annual Session

We send greetings from North Carolina Yearly Meeting (Friends United Meeting) from our 319th annual session. This year we gathered at Camp Caraway, nestled deep in the woods of Randolph County, in the Uwharrie Mountains, an excellent setting for our work of seeking God's will for the Yearly Meeting. Surrounded by the beauty of God's creation, 175 attenders from across the state, representing 51 Monthly Meetings used our time to listen and discern God's will.

For over two decades with increasing tensions over the last two years, we have wrestled with who we are, culminating in hurts, confusion, and financial challenges. This past year many of our meetings reaffirmed our faith in God, Jesus Christ, scripture, and our NCYM Faith and Practice. Regardless, a quarter of our monthly meetings have left North Carolina Yearly Meeting. We have heard of many yearly meetings and individuals who have prayed for us; we thank you.

Colin Saxton, General Secretary of Friends United Meeting, encouraged us in the opening worship session with the book of Acts. We tend to idealize early Friends, and the early church, forgetting that they also lived in the midst of theological arguments, political turmoil, poverty, and an unbelieving society. Colin challenged us to imagine an unhindered life and ministry as Paul did.

Committee reports, especially MOWA Choctaw, Quaker Lake Camp, Friends Disaster Service and Jamaica Ministries, demonstrated that we do have much in common as we share God's love as we serve others. We may use different words when we talk of God's saving action in our lives, but we speak a common language when serving others through God's love and call on our lives.

The gathered body continued to listen to Friends' concern about the direction of the yearly meeting, of whether or not to split, going our separate ways based on some arbitrary definition of "who we are." We heard a call for tolerance of others, meetings that seek to live the Love of God differently in service to their community. We heard that "we are already divided." Nineteen meetings have left the yearly meeting, and others are considering leaving the yearly meeting. We are splintering. Friends began to ask "Is intentional division better than unorganized splintering?" Everyone struggled to understand "authority" 'and "autonomy" and how to understand our life together in Christ. Is it better for NCYM-FUM to die to allow for a resurrection of a new organization? Could we serve Christ better if we reorganized our yearly meeting, our quarterly meetings, and our committees and ministries? Concerns were expressed about "Do we love one another, as Jesus teaches?" We were reminded of the words of Allen Jay over 100 years ago, "Separations have never brought one to Christ."

Due to theological differences, several meetings indicated that they would leave if the yearly meeting does not divide. Several other meetings spoke out against division. Out of the chaos and lack of clarity, in an effort to work with Love without compromising Faith, Friends approved a way to move forward. NCYM-FUM will work on reorganizing with subgroups or associations remaining under one yearly meeting umbrella. We intend to remain joined in essential ministries that are important to all, staying in relationship with each other, while we seek clarity of our theological distinctives for the groups that comprise the yearly meeting.

In the Saturday evening message, Colin Saxton reminded us that the Kingdom of God is in the deep places, not the shallow, easy-to-get-to places. We must have eyes to see, be willing to search. The Kingdom comes in glimpses and glimmers, but doors are always open.

We came here asking "Who has God called us to be? What has God called us to do?" We continue to discern these answers.

Our Life is Love: The Quaker Spiritual Journey. Marcelle Martin. San Francisco: Inner Light Books, 238 pages. Paperback, $17.50. Reviewed by Chuck Fager

It's my fate to spend a fair amount of time on the larger Quaker-oriented Facebook groups. That is often a challenging, and even dispiriting experience, especially when talk turns to "what Friends believe," and how that is evidenced in actual Quaker history. It's a chore because the level of ignorance and misinformation about Quakerism seems bottomless. Responding to it often is like bailing out a canoe with a big hole in the bottom, through which a continuing steam of errors, rumor, legends and downwright fiction steadily gushes.

For instance, a few days ago, there once again popped up the name of Richard Nixon, the second Quaker U. S. president. But no sooner than he appeared, there followed a number of firm denials that he was, or ever had been, a Friend. Even though Nixon's lifelong membership in East Whittier, California Friends Church is well-attested in several solid historical sources, both in books and online, this seemed to make no difference to many: pointing them out evoked such responses as: "He never was"; "Well, perhaps as a child, but not as an adult"; "Maybe as a young man, but when challenged as president over the Vietnam War, he left and never returned"; and other variations.

It's even worse when it comes to those things called "testimonies"; to read social media, one might think George Fox invented the Prius, or at least he drove one. And no doubt wore tee shirts emblazoned with "SPICE" (or was it "SPICES"?).

It's an uphill slog to point out that, oddly enough, when printed Books of Discipline appeared, about 1806, 120-plus years after Fox's death, and in many editions over several for decades, not only "Peace" but also "Equality," and even "Simplicity" were not found in their indexes or subject headings. (If one doubts, check this careful compilation of Old Disciplines here: http://www.qhpress.org/texts/obod/). To be sure, if one digs deep enough, seeds of some modern witness can be found in the rich humus of early Quaker writings; but as actual shoots of corporate expression they broke the surface only much later.

And there were counter-currents: for instance, while Quaker women could preach, travel as ministers, and had their own meetings, all of this was still subordinate to the men's meetings. And as for "equality," one ought to review Proposition 15 of Robert Barclay's *Apology* (also online, at:
http://www.qhpress.org/texts/barclay/apology/prop15.html), in particular the paragraph beginning, "Before I enter upon a particular disquisition . . ." in which he makes crystal clear that Friends' "peculiarities" about "hat honor," against bowing and scraping, and insisting on saying "thou" to a social superior – all this was to have absolutely **no** undermining effect on the inequality "betwixt prince and people, master and servants . . . **nay not at all**." Furthermore, "that these natural relations are rather **better established than any ways hurt** by it." (Emphasis added.)

But, but, sputter some, then whence cometh Quaker equality, if not from the tablets Fox carried down from atop Pendle Hill?

There's a double answer to that: first, things changed and evolved over 300 years. For instance, Fox and Penn accepted slavery; but over four generations, this acceptance became a definite refusal. And textually, Disciplines changed too, but even more slowly. Second, research thus far points the finger at the venerable Howard Brinton, and pamphlets he issued in 1941 and 1942, in which he listed equality, "harmony" (including peace) and simplicity as, not even "testimonies," but Quaker "social doctrines."

Further, Brinton acknowledged that his list had taken form, not full-blown, but after long experience and reflection – and some with no little struggle. He described these evolving "social doctrines" in his *Guide to Quaker Practice*, which is still in print, and has been, I am told, the best-selling Pendle Hill pamphlet in the 75 years since its issue. That durability and wide distribution evidently turned Brinton's rather tentative and qualified formulation into something of a liberal Quaker dogma. And forgetting the source, too many now assume that "social doctrines" equals "testimonies," and Brinton's list came direct from Firbank Fell and the First Publishers; one labors largely in vain to set them into a broader context, either of theology or history.

More formal presentations are hardly better. In 2011, the American Friends Service Committee produced a new pamphlet, sent to Meeting Clerks entitled, "An Introduction to Quaker Testimonies," which listed the "SPICES" version (The second "S" being for "Stewardship," a bow to the environment). This six-letter agenda is the most recent elaboration of Brinton's formulation, and it came printed on 100 per cent recycled paper – and it was also 100 % free of either historical framing or theological context.

So, besides continuing to wipe clear spots in the fogged-up windows of social media and organizational self-promotion, one would welcome any popular resource that might help Friends, old and new, find some clarity on these matters. And now comes, in this effort, *Our Life Is Love*, by Marcelle Martin.

In the book, which she says is based on long study and wide personal engagement, she draws on "acquaintance with the lives of seventeenth-century Quakers, combined with the experiences of dedicated Quakers today." From this mix she believes she has "unveiled ten essential elements in the process" of Quaker spiritual life. She chose the term "elements" carefully, insisting that the ten features are not to be taken as stages in a definite procession, or prescribed rungs on a spiritual ladder. Nevertheless, she begins from her own early sense of religious longing, as the first element, and the ten are grouped into three categories of Awakening, Convincement and Faithfulness, which certainly appear progressive, and reasonably so.

To illustrate her ten elements, she draws in quotes from numerous Friends, from early times and now. She also labors to include among them voices from across the theological spectrum and around the Quaker world, including Friends of color, Latin Americans and Africans. Linguistic and cultural differences make this effort feel strained at some points, but it's a noble one, and basic to developing a Quakerism for our time, and not just for our local parochial place.

The book is evidently attracting considerable attention in FGC-oriented Quaker circles. One Friend praised it to me as a surefire discussion starter in meeting reading-discussion groups. I can see that potential, and anything that can get Friends talking about actual Quakerism, in its past and present settings rather than their feelings about what are often no more than urban legends and rumors about it, is an asset.

At the same time, there are areas where the treatment of the elements was disappointing. Early Friends, for one, are typically presented as superhuman heroic and saintly figures. No doubt some were, at some times; yet from early on, the new movement also suffered through numerous internal conflicts and struggled with the impact of human imperfections. They included, to take only a few, Fox's seemingly ego-driven feud with James Nayler; William Penn's slaveowning; conflicts over removing hats during meeting, and even schism over setting definite times for meeting at all. Further, it took Fox years to quell fierce internal opposition to having women's meetings: Penn's "Primitive Christianity Revived" was by no means, a "Primitive Christianity of Equals."

For that matter, what we now call the "Peace Testimony" (in fact a much more recent usage) was by no means as clear and unequivocal then as many now would like to believe. Isaac Penington, who is one of this author's particular early role models (her title comes from him), was by no means a fan of pacifism. I don't say all this to denigrate early Friends; for me, learning of their feet of clay has only made them more real and accessible. But all that has no real place here.

From later times, Martin mentions the schisms that scattered the Society in the nineteenth century, but doesn't dwell on them. In one sense that is proper; this is not a history. Yet polarization and schism are by no means safely behind us. And there is essentially no mention here of the distressed condition of many Friends and meetings today, among whom some of the same forces are still tearing Quaker communities apart. This gives the text a parochial cast. It leaves one wondering if the author's many years of travel have brought her through any of those times of serious internal trouble, which are regrettably very much part of the Quaker experience today.

This lack gains importance when she speaks of "the Cross" as one of her elements. It surely belongs on such a list, but here too the book underplays a crucial aspect of the experience, that of group betrayal. After all, Jesus was sold out to the Romans by one of his inner circle. And in my time among Friends, those who seem most spiritually mature have borne scars that come not only from an unredeemed world, or from bold and costly witness, but also from within the circle of meeting, the community on which we depend. That hard experience of the cross is not really represented here, or at least not in any depth.

One other deficiency was that the book's admirable effort at inclusiveness seems to have missed both the large segments of non-mystic Friends, and the others gathered under the capacious umbrella of "non-theism." Such "mysto-chauvinism" is a common failing among both liberal Quakers and many otherwise progressive programmed Friends, too many of whom seem still to be following Rufus Jones and Howard Brinton in the belief that Quakerism is a kind of mystic sect, part of a fancied hidden "apostolic succession" of such groups that goes back presumably to Jesus himself. This notion has long since been thoroughly debunked by historians of religion; and its newest version, the evangelical "Holiness mysticism" of Carole Spencer, is no more convincing.

To be sure, Quakerism includes and perhaps produces mystics, as do many religions. Indeed, perhaps their presence, in measure, is indispensable to the health of the body. But Brinton-Jones-Spencer mysticism is much too narrow and dated a category to encompass all, or even all the greatest, Friends, then or now. Fox may have had "mystical experiences"; but he also had religious experiences of many other sorts, as recounted both in his *Journal* and the once-was-lost-but-now-it's-semi-found *Book of Miracles*. And many dedicated Quakers are like the British Friend William Littleboy, who exactly a century ago published "The Appeal of Quakerism for the Non-Mystic," a concise, classic apologia:

> "Can I who never consciously heard the inward voice," he wrote, "who am not of those to whom it is given to see visions and dream dreams – dare I believe that a real and intimate relationship exists between God and my own dull and earth-clogged soul? Upon the answer to our question stated in this personal form, depends I believe the hope and peace, the character of the whole outlook, of multitudes of anxious spirits. . . .
>
> God is above all the God of the normal. In the common facts and circumstances of life He draws near to us, quietly He teaches us in the routine of life's trifles, gently and unnoticed. His guidance comes to us through the channels of reason, judgment and determining circumstance.
>
> Exceptional experiences of revelation or guidance are not necessarily signs of deep spirituality. . . . We know that to some choice souls god's messages come in ways which are supernormal, and it is natural that we should look with longing eyes on these; yet such cases are the exception, not the rule."

(http://nontheists.quaker.org/CressonCadbury_10_27_03.pdf)

Note that Littleboy is not making his case as an agnostic nor non-theist. He is a believer, but of an undramatic, everyday sort. Nor was he lukewarm; he bore a strong witness for peace in World War One. And he is not alone. One of my Quaker heroes, Lucretia Mott, a faithful Friend her whole eighty-eight years, admired not only for eloquence but also physical courage, was likewise a resolutely anti-mystical Friend.

It's worth noting that Littleboy's plea is cited here by an advocate for non-theist Friends. They too deserve their place in Martin's book, but they do not find it. The book's Quaker vision is broad; it should be broader.

Fortunately, in today's publishing industry, a book is not, like Moses' tablets, carved in stone. It is relatively easy to update and enrich a text like this. I hope Martin and Inner Light Books will rise to that challenge, to make it all the resource it still could be.

For that matter, kudos are due to the publisher for producing a carefully-proofread text. This may seem a minor technical point; but it really isn't any more. The hunt for typographical errors used to be an almost religious rite, a quiet but relentless crusade for publishers and editors. But such attention to detail is vanishing, even from many eminent academic presses. Typos and other textual solecisms abound increasingly in books; and as an editor myself, I am mindful of my own shortcomings here. But this book was almost typo free; that bespeaks devotion as well as professionalsim, and deserves recognition and reinforcement.

With some further work, *Our Life Is Love* could reach its full potential. Perhaps– on can still hope– it could even help us tame and shed light in the wildlands of Quaker Facebook.

Quiet Heroes: A Century of American Quakers' Love and Help for the Japanese and Japanese-Americans. Tsukasa Sugimura. Intentional Productions. $20.00, paper. Reviewed by Chuck Fager

Want a good definition for "the middle of nowhere"? Try heading north on US highway 395, almost 120 miles past Death Valley in California, and 100-plus from the eastern entrance to Yosemite. This is the Owens Valley. It's home to bands of Paiute-Shoshone Indians, some hardy fruit farmers, cattle ranchers, and not much else on two legs. From here it's 336 miles to San Francisco, 226 to LA, and almost 250 to either Reno or Vegas. It's about the last place one would expect to find a Quaker landmark.

This is high desert, nearly 4000 feet, so it's hot in the summer, freezing and sometimes snowy in winter, and whipped by strong winds at any season. Twenty miles or so west are the Sierra Nevada mountains, often capped by snow and fantastic slow-swirling cloud formations. The area has been devastated by the long California drought.

It's the kind of place that quickly loses its scenic luster for me, and as a passenger riding north through it last spring, I drifted and dozed a lot.

I was about to doze again, as we passed through the tiny settlement of Lone Pine, when I saw a sign that snapped me fully awake: it bore one word: Manzanar.

I shouted that we had to stop, and shortly we did. Manzanar (it means "apple orchard" in Spanish) is now a national historic site, operated by the National

Park Service. It is where ten thousand Japanese-Americans were held as prisoners without charge or recourse for most of World War Two.

Inside, there are exhibits showing the outbreak of racism and war panic which led to the internment, and documentation of the harsh conditions the Nisei, as many were called, were subjected to. And there is a small gift shop, with a few shelves of books.

Quiet Heroes was on that shelf. The author, Tsukasa Sugimura, is the son of internees, who himself is now in his 60s. "Few know the story" here, he writes, " . . . the Japanese-Americans are aging, and with them, this valuable part of history is fading away."

He is so right. It's fading for Quakers too. When I took the book to the cash register, I asked the ranger there, "Do you know about Herbert Nicholson?"

She looked up, surprised. "Of course I do!" she said. And she called over the chief of the site.

Herbert Nicholson, they all knew, was one of the more memorable American Quakers who became involved in ministry to and advocacy for the interned Nisei. This was not a fluke, tho: although a Philadelphia Quaker by heritage, he had been evangelized by Billy Sunday, and spent twenty years in Japan as a missionary, sometimes with Quakers, sometimes with other groups.

Because he spoke English as well as Japanese, he had contacts who brought him information there beyond what the militarist Imperial government wanted people to know; and he spoke out against the growing war plans. This got him kicked out of Japan, and he landed in southern California, as pastor of a Japanese-American church. Then in early 1942, overnight, his congregation disappeared: they were hauled off to Manzanar or one of nine other isolated camps as far east as Arkansas.

Nicholson was shocked and enraged by the internment. He spent much of the next three years visiting the camps, ministering to those in them, and advocating for their release.

But as Sugimura shows, Nicholson was by no means the only Quaker in such work; Esther Rhoads, also a Philadelphian, was another. She too had been a missionary in Japan, and when she was likewise pushed out by the coming of war, she wound up working with the American Friends Service Committee, which was also very active in efforts on behalf of the Nisei.

AFSC's Executive Secretary Clarence Pickett also had more than a professional interest in these issues: his older sister had taught and worked in Japan for close to fifty years. As this suggests, Quaker work in Japan began long before the world war. In fact, it goes back to 1885, when one of the earliest Japanese Friends, Inazo Nitobe, visited Philadelphia and spoke to the very Orthodox women's mission board, and urged them to work for more education for women. The result was a girls school which is still in existence. (Nitobe had become Christian in Japan, then joined Friends in

Baltimore Yearly Meeting while studying at Johns Hopkins University.)

Nitobe was also a pioneer in another way: while studying at Johns Hopkins University, he met and courted Friend Mary Elkinton. They became engaged, but both her parents and their meeting elders objected; the stated reason was that the marriage would take Mary to Japan, far away. But one suspects that race was also involved. Nonetheless, the couple patiently but doggedly worked to change the minds of both parents and meeting elders, and were married in 1890. This is a love story that deserves much fuller treatment than seems to be available now.

Quakers did not become numerous in Japan, but were active in important work, particularly after earthquakes and other natural disasters. Nitobe and others also labored to maintain peace between Japan and the United States. In the short term, they failed, as the calamity of World War and the horror of the atomic bomb showed. Yet their work continued. Esther Rhoads and another Philadelphian, Elizabeth Gray Vining, became tutors of the crown prince after World War Two, and helped inculcate peace values in the young man which persist even in his late years today.

A native Japanese-American Quaker, Gordon Hirabayashi, served three months in prison in the U.S. for violating a 1942 curfew specially imposed on citizens with his background. He fought that case to the Supreme Court and lost. Many years later, after a long legal struggle, he was able to reopen the case, and the Supreme Court reversed itself. "The U. S. government admitted it made a mistake," Hirabayashi said afterward. President Obama awarded him the Medal of Freedom in 2012, unfortunately a few months after his death at 93.

Author Sugimura is not a historian, but rather a pastor in a mainly Japanese-American church in California. He touches on all this history, but his main focus is on the work of Friends with the interned Nisei in camps like Manzanar during the war. His reading has been broad and diligent, and his footnotes, more than 170, include a listing of many obscure but important books and other records of this larger saga. It deserves a fuller account, but Sugimura's compact volume can serve to open up the field.

And if readers off *Quiet Heroes* ever find themselves on US highway 395 in Owens Valley, California, they should keep an eye open when headed north from Lone Pine, because soon they'll see, there in what seems like the middle of nowhere, the sign for an unlikely but momentous and very enriching landmark for Quakers, and many others too; don't miss it.

Manzanar study site:
https://www.nps.gov/nr/twhp/wwwlps/lessons/89manzanar/89setting.htm

Blog post: http://wp.me/p5FGIu-1Lc

About the Contributors

Ken Bradstock has been a U.S. Marine, a deputy sheriff, and for many years, a hospice counselor. He is also the Clerk of Fancy Gap Friends meeting in Ararat, Virginia.

Chuck Fager is the Editor of Quaker Theology. His most recent book is *Meetings: A Religious Autobiography.*

H. Larry Ingle is retired from teaching hisory at the University of Tennessee-Chattanooga. His most recent book is *Nixon's First Cover-Up*, from the University of Missouri Press, about the former president's long concealment and obfuscation of his Quaker membership and identity.

Jacob Stone is a longtime member of Doylestown Monthly Meeting (PhYM). He is now living in retirement in Montpelier, Vermont after a long career in human services and human services education at Marywood University and The University of Alaska Fairbanks, as well as serving as an ethicist and ethics trainer. He and his wife Gretta have served as Friends in Residence at Pendle Hill and at Chena Ridge Meeting in Fairbanks, Alaska, and as Co-Directors for five years at Ben Lomond Quaker Center in California. They have also been leading couple enrichment events for twenty one years.

Put *Quaker Theology* In Your Mailbox –
And your Meeting Library:

A subscription to *Quaker Theology* will be a valuable addition to the reading matter of Friends meetings and schools. It will also help support our ongoing work of sustaining a progressive journal and forum for discussion and study. It's economical too.

Will you pass this form on to your Library Committee? Or better yet, make a gift of a subscription to your meeting?

Thank Thee!

Please enter a subscription to *Quaker Theology*

____1 year (two issues) $20

____2 years (four issues) $35

(Overseas subscribers: US$30 per year.)

NAME_____

ADDRESS:_____

_____Zip/Post Code_____

Send this form and payment to:

Quaker Theology
P.O. Box 3811
Durham NC 27702

Quaker Theology – There's Nothing Else Like It.

Made in the USA
San Bernardino, CA
19 September 2016